The Programmer's Insight

Seeing the Unseen in Code

Georgie Skeldon

The Programmers Insight 1
Seeing the Unseen in Code 1
Georgie Skeldon 1
Chapter 1: The Mindset of Code Perception 5
    Training Your Programming Intuition 5
    Pattern Recognition in Software 9
    Developing Code Reading Fluency 13
    The Art of Mental Modeling 17
    Bridging Abstract and Concrete Thinking 21
Chapter 2: Hidden Structures and Relationships 27
    Architectural Patterns Beyond Design 27
    Data Flow Visualization 31
    Understanding Code Dependencies 36
Chapter 3: Debugging as Investigation 41
    Reading Error Signatures 41
    Tracing System Behavior 45
    Root Cause Analysis 50
    Performance Bottleneck Detection 55
    Debugging Mindset and Methodology 60
Chapter 4: Code Evolution and Maintenance 65
    Identifying Technical Debt 65
    Recognizing Refactoring Opportunities 69
    Legacy Code Navigation 74
    Change Impact Analysis 78
Chapter 5: System Level Understanding 84
    Component Interaction Patterns 84
    Resource Management Insights 89
    Scalability Indicators 94
    Security Vulnerability Recognition 99

 Integration Point Analysis 104
Chapter 6: The Human Element in Code 110
 Reading Developer Intent 110
 Code Style as Communication 114
 Documentation Psychology 118
Chapter 7: Future Proofing and Innovation 123
 Emerging Pattern Detection 123
 Extensibility Assessment 127
 Technology Evolution Awareness 132
 Adaptation Strategies 136
 Innovation Opportunities 141

Chapter 1: The Mindset of Code Perception

Training Your Programming Intuition

Programming intuition is not a skill bestowed upon a select few but rather a cultivated ability developed over time through deliberate practice and mindful observation. It is the innate sense that allows seasoned developers to anticipate potential issues, foresee solutions, and navigate codebases with a level of comfort that appears effortless. This ability is not magical but emerges from an amalgamation of experience, pattern recognition, and a deep understanding of fundamental concepts. To train such intuition, one must first dismantle the illusion that programming is purely logical and embrace its inherently creative and interpretive nature.

At its core, programming intuition begins with familiarity. Immersing oneself in a variety of codebases is an essential practice. The more you expose yourself to different styles, structures, and paradigms, the more you begin to internalize patterns and approaches. Over time, these patterns become second nature, allowing you to instinctively recognize what works and what doesn't. A novice programmer may struggle to understand why a particular algorithm is more efficient, but an experienced one intuitively knows where inefficiencies might lie, even before running performance tests. This sense comes from repeatedly encountering similar problems and observing their solutions in action.

Another key aspect of developing programming intuition is to focus on the "why" behind the code. It's not enough to know how a piece of code functions; understanding the motivation and reasoning behind its implementation is what truly deepens intuition. When reading through a codebase, ask yourself: why was this particular approach chosen? What constraints or requirements might have influenced this decision? By engaging with the thought process of the original developer, you begin to align your mental models with theirs, bridging gaps in understanding and honing your ability to anticipate similar decisions in the future.

Mistakes, too, are invaluable teachers. Errors and bugs, while often frustrating, are opportunities to refine your instincts. When debugging, resist the urge to immediately search for solutions. Instead, take the time to dissect the issue, hypothesize possible causes, and trace the flow of the program methodically. Each debugging session is a lesson in problem-solving that strengthens your ability to predict where things might go wrong. Over time, a seasoned developer can often spot potential pitfalls in code even before they manifest, a skill rooted in countless hours of debugging and troubleshooting.

Programming intuition also involves an element of abstraction. A strong programmer doesn't get lost in the minutiae of syntax or the specifics of a particular language but instead approaches problems conceptually. They see beyond the lines of code to the architecture and logic that underpin it. Training yourself to think at this level requires deliberate practice. Start by breaking down complex problems into their fundamental components. What is the problem asking? What are the inputs and outputs? What are the constraints? By stripping away extraneous details, you can focus on the essence of the problem, allowing you to devise cleaner and more effective solutions.

Code reviews are another powerful tool for building intuition. Reviewing others' code exposes you to different ways of thinking and problem-solving. It forces you to critically analyze approaches and evaluate their strengths and weaknesses. Over time, you begin to recognize common patterns and anti-patterns, sharpening your ability to assess code quality instinctively. Likewise, inviting others to critique your code can reveal blind spots in your thinking and challenge your assumptions, further refining your skills.

It's also important to embrace the iterative nature of programming. Rarely is the first solution the best solution. Intuition often emerges through the process of refining and optimizing code. As you revisit and improve upon your work, you begin to notice subtleties and nuances that may have eluded you initially. This iterative process not only results in better code but also sharpens your ability to identify areas for improvement in future projects.

Exposure to diverse programming paradigms and languages is another critical factor. Each paradigm— whether procedural, object-oriented, functional, or declarative—offers unique perspectives and tools for problem-solving. By learning multiple paradigms, you expand your mental toolkit, enabling you to approach problems from different angles. Similarly, exploring different languages can reveal new idioms and constructs that challenge and expand your thinking. While it's not necessary to master every language, familiarity with a variety of them broadens your perspective and enhances your adaptability.

Reading technical literature, blogs, and documentation further deepens your understanding and intuition. These resources often provide insights into best practices, common pitfalls, and innovative approaches that you can incorporate into your own work. Additionally, many experienced developers share their thought processes and lessons learned, offering valuable glimpses into how they approach problems. By engaging with such materials, you can accelerate your learning and gain insights that might otherwise take years to acquire through experience alone.

Lastly, cultivating programming intuition requires a mindset of curiosity and continuous learning. Technology is constantly evolving, and staying current is essential. Attend meetups, participate in hackathons, and engage with the broader programming community. These interactions expose you to new ideas and approaches while keeping you inspired and motivated. Remember, intuition is not a static trait but a dynamic ability that grows and evolves with experience and exposure.

The journey to developing programming intuition is a gradual one, marked by persistence and practice. It is a process of accumulating knowledge, internalizing patterns, and refining your mental models. While the path may be challenging, the rewards are immense, enabling you to navigate the complexities of programming with confidence and ease.

Pattern Recognition in Software

Pattern recognition in software is a cornerstone of effective programming, enabling developers to identify recurring concepts, structures, and solutions within complex systems. It is not merely a technical skill but a way of thinking that transforms how one approaches problems, interprets code, and devises solutions. At its essence, pattern recognition is about seeing the underlying order in what might initially appear chaotic. This cognitive ability allows programmers to navigate unfamiliar codebases, design scalable systems, and write maintainable code with remarkable efficiency.

Recognizing patterns begins with an awareness of the recurring elements within software systems. These patterns often manifest as design patterns, architectural paradigms, or algorithmic strategies. For example, the observer pattern frequently appears in event-driven systems, while the singleton pattern is often used to manage shared resources. Familiarity with these patterns equips you with a mental library of solutions to common problems. When faced with a new challenge, you can draw on this library, recognizing parallels between the current situation and those you have encountered before. This recognition is not a rote application of patterns but a deeper understanding of their purpose and context.

Beyond formal design patterns, programming is rich with informal patterns that reflect how humans solve problems. Consider the way loops and conditionals are structured, or how data is passed between functions. Over time, you begin to notice the subtle consistencies in how developers approach these tasks, even across different languages and frameworks. These consistencies form the foundation for intuition, allowing you to predict how a given piece of code might behave or how a problem might best be approached. For instance, seasoned developers often anticipate the use of caching mechanisms in performance-critical applications or recognize the need for modularity in systems expected to scale.

Pattern recognition is not limited to static code but extends to dynamic behaviors and interactions. Observing how data flows through a system, how components interact, or how users engage with software reveals patterns that inform design and debugging. For example, recognizing a bottleneck in data processing might lead you to implement parallel processing patterns. Similarly, noticing repetitive user actions could inspire the creation of shortcuts or automation features. These insights arise not from isolated observations but from identifying trends and correlations over time.

Developing the ability to recognize patterns requires deliberate practice and exposure. Immersing yourself in diverse codebases is one of the most effective ways to cultivate this skill. Each codebase introduces you to new approaches, idioms, and conventions, broadening your perspective and enriching your mental library of patterns. The more varied your experience, the more adaptable and versatile your pattern recognition becomes. This adaptability is crucial, as patterns often appear in slightly altered forms depending on the context, and rigid thinking can hinder your ability to identify them.

Another critical aspect of pattern recognition is understanding the trade-offs and limitations of each pattern. No solution is universally applicable, and blindly applying a pattern without considering its implications can lead to suboptimal results. For example, while the use of global variables might seem convenient in small scripts, it can lead to maintainability issues in larger systems. Recognizing when a pattern is appropriate—and when it is not—is a hallmark of expertise. This discernment comes from experience and a willingness to reflect on past decisions, learning from both successes and mistakes.

Collaboration and communication also play a significant role in honing pattern recognition. Engaging with peers through code reviews, pair programming, or technical discussions exposes you to alternative viewpoints and approaches. These interactions challenge your assumptions and encourage you to think critically about your own patterns of thought. Moreover, explaining your reasoning to others forces you to articulate and clarify your understanding, deepening your awareness of the patterns you rely on.

Pattern recognition extends beyond individual projects to encompass broader industry trends and best practices. Staying informed about emerging technologies, frameworks, and methodologies keeps your mental library current and relevant. For instance, the rise of microservices architecture reflects a shift toward patterns that prioritize scalability and resilience. Recognizing these trends allows you to anticipate the direction of industry developments and position yourself to adapt effectively.

The human brain is naturally wired for pattern recognition, but sharpening this ability in the context of software development requires intentional effort. One practical approach is to regularly analyze and refactor your own code. Look for redundancies, inconsistencies, or areas where a more elegant solution might exist. This process not only improves the quality of your work but also trains your eye to identify patterns more readily. Similarly, studying the work of more experienced developers can provide valuable insights into how they structure their code and solve problems.

Pattern recognition is as much about creativity as it is about logic. It involves connecting disparate pieces of information, drawing parallels between seemingly unrelated concepts, and envisioning possibilities beyond the immediate problem at hand. This creative aspect is what makes programming both challenging and rewarding. While the technical details of syntax and algorithms are essential, it is the ability to see the bigger picture, to discern the patterns that shape software, that distinguishes great programmers from merely competent ones.

Developing Code Reading Fluency

Reading code fluently is an essential skill for any programmer, yet it is often overlooked in favor of writing code. The ability to seamlessly navigate, interpret, and understand code written by others—or even by your past self—can make the difference between a developer who struggles to maintain existing systems and one who confidently builds on them. Fluency in reading code is not simply about deciphering syntax or understanding what the program does. It's about grasping the intent behind the code, recognizing patterns, and visualizing the flow of logic. This skill grows through consistent practice, exposure, and a structured approach to dissecting unfamiliar codebases.

The first step to developing fluency in reading code is approaching it with a mindset of curiosity rather than judgment. Code, like written language, reflects the personality, experience level, and thought process of its author. Some code may appear elegant and intuitive, while other parts might seem convoluted or unnecessarily complex. Rather than becoming frustrated by poorly written or confusing code, view it as an opportunity to learn. Often, by digging into the reasons behind certain decisions, you uncover valuable insights into the challenges faced by the original developer or the constraints of the system at the time.

When faced with unfamiliar code, it's important to start with the broader context before diving into the details. Understanding the purpose of the codebase as a whole can provide critical clues about how individual components are designed and why they function as they do. Begin by exploring the documentation, comments, and any architecture diagrams available. If none exist, take a step back and examine the directory structure, naming conventions, and entry points to piece together an initial mental model of the system. This high-level understanding serves as a map, guiding you as you delve deeper into the code.

An effective way to build fluency is by tracing the execution path of the program. Following the flow of logic from one function or module to another helps you understand how the pieces fit together. Start with the entry point, such as the main function or the primary script that initiates the program. From there, follow the calls and references step by step, observing how data is passed, transformed, and utilized. Take note of key variables, parameters, and return values, as these often reveal the core operations of the code. Tracing the execution path not only demystifies the immediate functionality but also strengthens your ability to infer relationships between different parts of the system.

Another crucial aspect of code reading fluency is pattern recognition. With experience, you begin to notice recurring idioms, frameworks, and structures within the code. For instance, a seasoned developer might immediately recognize a common authentication flow, a pagination implementation, or a caching mechanism. These familiar patterns act as shortcuts, allowing you to understand substantial portions of the code at a glance. Cultivating this skill requires exposure to a wide variety of codebases, as each one adds to your mental library of patterns and conventions.

Even the best-written code can be daunting without a strategy for breaking it into manageable pieces. When encountering large or complex files, resist the urge to tackle everything at once. Instead, break the code into logical sections and focus on understanding one piece at a time. Look for natural boundaries, such as function definitions, classes, or modules. Pay special attention to the interfaces—how one section interacts with another—because these connections often reveal the purpose and scope of each component. By systematically working through the code, you reduce the cognitive load and make the task more approachable.

Comments and documentation, when present, can be invaluable tools for understanding code. However, it's important to approach them critically. Not all comments are accurate, up-to-date, or helpful. Use them as a starting point, but always verify their claims by studying the code itself. Similarly, naming conventions can provide subtle hints about the intent and functionality of variables, functions, or classes. Descriptive names often tell a story about the code's purpose, while inconsistent or ambiguous names might signal areas that require closer inspection.

Reading fluency also involves developing an eye for the small details that reveal the developer's intent. Subtle decisions, such as the choice of a particular data structure or algorithm, can speak volumes about the goals and constraints of the code. For instance, the use of a hash table instead of a list might indicate a focus on fast lookup times, while the presence of a recursive function suggests a hierarchical or tree-like structure to the data. By paying attention to these choices, you gain insight into the reasoning behind the code, which in turn informs your own understanding and decision-making.

Practicing code reviews is one of the most effective ways to improve your reading fluency. Reviewing someone else's code forces you to engage with their thought process, analyze their decisions, and identify areas for improvement. It challenges you to articulate your observations clearly and provides feedback that sharpens your skills. Similarly, inviting others to review your code can expose you to alternative perspectives and highlight blind spots in your understanding.

Fluency in reading code is not only about understanding what the code does but also about anticipating potential pitfalls and areas for improvement. As you read, constantly ask yourself questions: Is this code efficient? Is it maintainable? Are there edge cases that might break the logic? This habit of critical analysis transforms code reading from a passive exercise into an active and engaging process. Over time, you develop the ability to quickly assess the quality and reliability of code, a skill that is invaluable for debugging, optimization, and collaborative development.

The journey to becoming fluent in reading code is a continuous one. Each new codebase you encounter, each review you perform, and each problem you solve contributes to your growth. It is a skill that evolves alongside your programming expertise, enabling you to tackle increasingly complex systems with confidence and clarity. By committing to practice and maintaining a sense of curiosity, you can transform what might initially feel like a daunting task into one of the most rewarding aspects of software development.

The Art of Mental Modeling

Mental modeling is an essential skill in programming, a cognitive framework that allows developers to visualize, predict, and understand the intricate systems they build and interact with. It is the bridge between abstract concepts and concrete implementations, providing clarity in chaos and a structured way to approach seemingly insurmountable challenges. At its core, mental modeling is about creating a representation of how a system works in your mind, enabling you to navigate its complexities with confidence and precision.

When approaching a problem, the first step in constructing an effective mental model is understanding the system's purpose. Every piece of software is designed to solve a problem, fulfill a need, or provide a service. By identifying the system's goals, you begin to outline its boundaries and key components. For example, consider a web application designed for e-commerce. Its purpose is not just to display products but also to manage user authentication, handle transactions securely, and maintain inventory records. Recognizing these objectives allows you to start visualizing the relationships between different parts of the system.

Breaking a system into smaller, digestible components is vital for building a clear mental model. Large systems can be overwhelming, but when divided into modules or layers, they become more manageable. Think of it like dissecting a machine: instead of trying to understand every gear, wire, and switch simultaneously, you focus on one subsystem at a time. For instance, in a web application, you might focus on the front-end interface first, then move on to the back-end logic, and finally examine the database interactions. This step-by-step approach not only simplifies the process but also reveals how each part contributes to the system as a whole.

Relationships between components are at the heart of mental modeling. Understanding how data flows, how processes communicate, and how dependencies are structured is critical. Consider a messaging application. Messages originate from the user interface, are sent to a server, processed, and then relayed to a recipient. Each of these steps represents a distinct component, but the flow of data between them forms the connective tissue of the system. Visualizing this flow helps you anticipate bottlenecks, pinpoint potential failure points, and understand the overall architecture.

Dynamic aspects of a system, such as state changes and interactions, add another layer of complexity to mental modeling. Static models, like diagrams or flowcharts, can be helpful, but they often fail to capture how a system evolves over time. Take, for instance, a traffic control system. At any given moment, traffic lights, sensors, and control algorithms are interacting in real-time. To model this effectively, you need to envision not just the components but also their behaviors, triggers, and responses. Techniques like state machines and sequence diagrams can aid in representing these dynamic aspects, but the key lies in mentally simulating the system's operation.

Experience plays a significant role in refining mental models. The more systems you analyze and work with, the more adept you become at recognizing patterns and abstractions. For example, a developer who has worked on numerous database-driven applications will likely have an intuitive grasp of concepts like normalization, indexing, and query optimization. This familiarity allows them to construct mental models more quickly and accurately. However, it's important to remain adaptable. No two systems are identical, and applying preconceived notions without considering the unique characteristics of a system can lead to flawed assumptions.

Misconceptions are a common pitfall in mental modeling. It's easy to infer a relationship or behavior that doesn't actually exist, leading to errors and confusion. To counteract this, always validate your assumptions. Test your understanding by tracing specific scenarios through the system or by discussing your model with peers. Collaboration often reveals gaps or inaccuracies in your thinking, providing an opportunity to refine and improve your model. Additionally, documentation can serve as a valuable reference for verifying details and ensuring alignment with the actual implementation.

Mental modeling is not limited to software systems; it extends to workflows, teams, and even the development process itself. For instance, when managing a team of developers, constructing a mental model of how tasks flow from requirement gathering to deployment can help identify inefficiencies or bottlenecks. Similarly, understanding the dependencies and interactions within a project timeline allows you to anticipate challenges and allocate resources effectively. These broader applications of mental modeling underscore its versatility and importance in every aspect of programming.

Visualization is a powerful tool in mental modeling. While much of the process occurs in your mind, external representations like diagrams, sketches, or whiteboard sessions can help crystallize your thoughts. For example, drawing a data flow diagram for a content management system might reveal redundancies or missing connections that were not immediately apparent. These visual aids serve as extensions of your mental model, making it easier to communicate your understanding to others and to revisit and refine your model as new information becomes available.

Iteration is a natural part of developing and maintaining mental models. As systems evolve, so too must your understanding of them. A model that was accurate at the beginning of a project may become outdated as new features are added, technologies are changed, or requirements shift. Regularly revisiting and updating your mental model ensures that it remains relevant and useful. This iterative process also reinforces your understanding, deepening your expertise over time.

The art of mental modeling lies in its balance between abstraction and detail. Too much abstraction can obscure critical nuances, while too much detail can overwhelm and confuse. Striking the right balance requires practice and a keen awareness of the context in which you are working. For example, when debugging a specific issue, a highly detailed model of the affected components may be necessary. In contrast, when presenting a system overview to stakeholders, a more abstract model will likely suffice.

Bridging Abstract and Concrete Thinking

Abstract and concrete thinking are two complementary modes of reasoning that, when effectively bridged, allow programmers to navigate the complexities of software development. Abstract thinking is the ability to conceptualize overarching ideas, identify patterns, and envision systems at a high level. It concerns itself with the "why" and "what"—the purpose and logic behind a system. Concrete thinking, on the other hand, focuses on the specific implementation details, the "how" of translating those ideas into functioning code. Bridging these two modes is essential for creating robust, scalable systems that are both conceptually sound and practically executable.

Every successful software project begins with a degree of abstraction. Before writing a single line of code, developers engage in high-level thinking to define the problem, outline goals, and envision potential solutions. This process often involves identifying the core components of a system and how they interact. For instance, when designing an e-commerce platform, you might initially think about the major entities involved: customers, products, orders, and payments. At this stage, you're not concerned with database schemas or API endpoints. Instead, you're constructing a mental framework that captures the essence of the system. This abstraction serves as a foundation on which the concrete details will later be built.

Abstract thinking also plays a critical role in identifying patterns and reusability. Experienced developers often recognize when a problem resembles one they've solved before, whether it's handling user authentication, managing data storage, or implementing search functionality. By thinking abstractly, they can generalize these solutions into reusable components or frameworks that can be applied across projects. This ability to step back and see the bigger picture is what enables efficient problem-solving and innovation.

However, abstraction alone is not enough. Without grounding these ideas in concrete implementation, they remain theoretical and disconnected from reality. The transition from abstract to concrete thinking begins by breaking down high-level concepts into actionable tasks. Take, for example, the concept of user authentication. At an abstract level, you understand that users need a secure way to log in and manage their accounts. To bring this idea to life, you must consider practical questions: What data will be stored? Will passwords be hashed, and if so, using which algorithm? How will session management be handled? These specific decisions translate abstract goals into tangible outcomes.

Concrete thinking thrives on precision. It demands attention to detail, whether it's writing clean code, debugging errors, or optimizing performance. When implementing a feature, every line of code must serve a purpose and align with the overall design. This level of focus ensures that the abstract vision is faithfully executed without unnecessary complexity or deviation. For instance, when implementing an API endpoint to retrieve product details, you must consider the input parameters, error handling, and response format. These specifics may seem mundane compared to the grander vision, but they are the building blocks that make the system functional and reliable.

The process of bridging abstract and concrete thinking is not linear but iterative. As you delve into the details of implementation, you may uncover limitations or challenges that prompt you to revisit and refine your abstract ideas. For example, a high-level plan to use a relational database for storing user data might seem straightforward at first. Yet, during implementation, you might realize that the structure needs to accommodate complex relationships or scale differently than anticipated. This feedback loop ensures that the abstract and concrete aspects of your work remain aligned and mutually informed.

One of the common pitfalls in bridging these two modes of thinking is becoming stuck in one at the expense of the other. Over-reliance on abstraction can lead to designs that are elegant on paper but impractical to implement. Conversely, focusing solely on concrete details can result in fragmented systems that lack cohesion and fail to address the broader problem. Balancing the two requires discipline and a willingness to switch perspectives as needed. When faced with a challenge, ask yourself whether you're thinking too abstractly or too concretely. Adjusting your approach can often reveal new insights and solutions.

Collaboration is another key factor in bridging abstract and concrete thinking. Within a development team, individuals often bring different strengths to the table. Some excel at high-level planning and system design, while others are skilled at writing efficient, detailed code. By working together, these diverse perspectives can create a more seamless transition between the abstract and the concrete. For instance, a software architect might outline the overall design of a microservices system, while individual developers focus on implementing specific services. Regular communication ensures that the work remains cohesive and aligned with the overarching goals.

Documentation also plays a vital role in bridging these modes of thought. High-level documentation, such as architecture diagrams and requirement specifications, provides a reference point for abstract thinking. Detailed documentation, such as API references and code comments, supports concrete implementation. Together, they create a shared understanding that guides the development process from concept to execution. A well-documented project is easier to navigate, reducing the cognitive load required to switch between abstract and concrete perspectives.

Another powerful tool is prototyping. Prototypes serve as a bridge between the abstract and the concrete, allowing you to test ideas before committing to a full implementation. For example, building a simple mockup of a user interface can help you validate whether your design aligns with user needs. Similarly, creating a basic proof-of-concept for a back-end service can reveal potential technical challenges early on. Prototyping provides a tangible way to explore abstract ideas, ensuring that they are grounded in practical feasibility.

The ability to move fluidly between abstract and concrete thinking is a skill that develops with experience. It requires practice, reflection, and a willingness to learn from both successes and failures. Over time, you become more adept at recognizing when to zoom out and focus on the big picture, and when to zoom in and address the finer details. This adaptability is what enables developers to tackle complex problems, build scalable systems, and create software that not only works but also serves its intended purpose elegantly.

Bridging these two modes of thinking is not just a technical exercise but a creative one. It involves synthesizing ideas, balancing competing priorities, and navigating uncertainty. By mastering this interplay, you equip yourself with the tools to approach any project with clarity, confidence, and ingenuity. It is this balance between the abstract and the concrete that lies at the heart of effective and meaningful software development.

Chapter 2: Hidden Structures and Relationships

Architectural Patterns Beyond Design

Architectural patterns are often associated with system design stages, where high-level decisions shape the foundation of a software project. But their influence extends far beyond initial design; they are living entities that evolve alongside a system as it grows, adapts, and ages. Understanding these patterns in their broader context means not only recognizing their structural implications but also appreciating their role in guiding development, fostering collaboration, and addressing long-term challenges. They are the scaffolding that supports not just the code itself but the organization and processes that surround it.

At their essence, architectural patterns provide blueprints for solving recurrent problems in software development. They define how components of a system interact, communicate, and function as a cohesive whole. Patterns like layered architecture, microservices, event-driven systems, or monolithic designs are not merely technical constructs; they embody philosophies about how to manage complexity, performance, and maintainability. Recognizing the principles behind these patterns helps developers make informed decisions that align with the needs of their systems over time, rather than locking them into a rigid structure that becomes a liability.

Take the layered architecture, for example. It's a classic choice for many applications, dividing functionality into distinct layers such as presentation, business logic, and data access. At first glance, its purpose seems clear: to separate concerns and promote modularity. But over time, a deeper understanding of its role emerges. The layered approach not only simplifies the development process but also impacts testing, scaling, and team organization. By isolating layers, you can test each independently, ensuring robust functionality at every level. Similarly, dividing responsibilities allows scaling to happen at specific layers, such as adding caching mechanisms to the data layer for improved performance.

Yet, architectural patterns are not static prescriptions. They must evolve with the system's requirements. A layered architecture that works well for a small application might begin to show strain as the codebase grows. Over time, tight coupling between layers or inefficient data flows can emerge, requiring refactoring or adjustments. This is where the true power of architectural patterns lies—not in their initial implementation, but in their adaptability. Recognizing when and how to evolve your architecture is a skill that separates experienced developers from novices.

Microservices, another widely discussed architectural pattern, illustrate the dynamic nature of these decisions. At their core, microservices break down a system into independent, loosely coupled services that communicate through well-defined APIs. This approach offers clear benefits like scalability, fault isolation, and the ability to use different technologies for different services. However, as systems mature, the challenges of microservices become apparent. Managing service communication, deploying updates without breaking dependencies, and monitoring dozens or hundreds of services require careful consideration. While the initial design might focus on the technical implementation, the long-term success of a microservices architecture depends on how well it supports organizational workflows and operational demands.

Event-driven architectures highlight another dimension of architectural patterns: their impact on system behavior over time. By decoupling services through asynchronous events, these systems promote scalability and resilience, allowing different components to evolve independently. However, the trade-offs include increased complexity in debugging and the potential for cascading failures if one event triggers a chain reaction. Appreciating these nuances requires looking beyond the design phase and considering how the architecture will behave under real-world conditions, such as high traffic, unexpected errors, or changes in business requirements.

One of the most overlooked aspects of architectural patterns is their influence on team dynamics. The way a software system is structured often mirrors the communication patterns of the team building it. Known as Conway's Law, this principle suggests that organizational structures and software architectures are deeply intertwined. A monolithic architecture might work well for a small, tightly-knit team where everyone has a shared understanding of the system. In contrast, a microservices approach aligns better with larger teams, where different groups can take ownership of individual services. Recognizing this relationship helps ensure that the architecture supports, rather than hinders, collaboration and productivity.

Another dimension to consider is the lifecycle of architectural patterns. As systems age, their architectures become more susceptible to technical debt. What once seemed like a well-thought-out design can gradually become brittle and inflexible. This is particularly true for patterns that rely on specific technologies or assumptions that may no longer hold true. For instance, a system designed around a relational database might struggle to adapt to the demands of real-time analytics or large-scale data processing. Regularly revisiting and reevaluating architectural decisions ensures that they continue to meet the system's objectives and remain aligned with current realities.

Scalability is often cited as a primary concern in architectural decisions, but it is not the only measure of success. Resilience, maintainability, and extensibility are equally important factors. A well-designed architecture should not only handle increased load but also recover gracefully from failures, accommodate new features with minimal disruption, and evolve to meet changing user needs. This requires a forward-thinking mindset that goes beyond simply implementing a pattern and instead focuses on how it will support the system's growth and change over time.

One of the challenges in working with architectural patterns is striking the right balance between abstraction and specificity. Patterns provide guidance, but they are not one-size-fits-all solutions. Applying a pattern without understanding its context or tailoring it to your specific needs can lead to inefficiencies and complications. For example, adopting a microservices architecture for a simple application with low traffic might introduce unnecessary complexity without delivering significant benefits. On the other hand, over-customizing a pattern can make it harder to maintain or scale. The key lies in understanding the trade-offs and making deliberate, informed decisions.

Documentation plays a critical role in ensuring that architectural patterns remain effective throughout a system's lifecycle. High-level diagrams, detailed descriptions of component interactions, and clear explanations of design choices provide a reference point for future developers. This documentation not only helps newcomers understand the system but also supports ongoing maintenance and evolution. Without it, even the most elegant architecture can become a tangled web as changes accumulate over time.

Data Flow Visualization

Understanding how data moves through a system is a pivotal aspect of software development. Data flow visualization acts as a lens through which developers can perceive the interconnections, pathways, and transformations of information within a system. This practice is more than just a technical exercise; it is a narrative tool, one that allows developers to tell the story of the system, revealing the relationships between inputs, processes, and outputs in a way that transcends raw code. When done effectively, it provides clarity, fosters collaboration, and unveils inefficiencies or bottlenecks that might otherwise remain hidden.

The foundation of data flow visualization begins with mapping the journey of data from its origin to its final destination. Every system has its entry points, whether a user submitting a form, a sensor transmitting data, or an external API delivering information. Tracing this data as it traverses through various layers—processing, storage, and output—requires a comprehensive understanding of the system's architecture. For instance, in a content management system, data might originate from a user uploading an image, get processed for resizing and metadata extraction, and eventually be stored in a database while being displayed on the front end. Mapping such flows not only helps with understanding system behavior but also serves as a guide for debugging and optimizing performance.

Visualization tools and techniques enable developers to externalize these flows, transforming abstract concepts into tangible representations. Diagrams are often the most straightforward and effective method. A data flow diagram can represent processes as nodes, with arrows indicating the movement of data between them. The simplicity of such diagrams belies their power; they offer a bird's-eye view of the system, making it easy to identify redundant processes, unclear dependencies, or unnecessary complexity. For instance, a developer examining a diagram of a payment processing system might immediately notice that data is being redundantly validated at multiple points, prompting a re-evaluation of the design.

Colors, shapes, and annotations can further enhance these visualizations. Highlighting specific pathways—such as those related to critical transactions or high-volume data streams—draws attention to areas that require priority in terms of optimization or monitoring. For example, in a distributed system, visualizing the flow of data across nodes in different geographic locations can reveal latency issues or overburdened network segments. Annotations in the diagram can provide context, such as indicating specific APIs, data formats, or expected processing times, adding layers of detail that aid in decision-making and troubleshooting.

Beyond diagrams, interactive dashboards and tools have become increasingly popular for real-time data flow visualization. These tools not only depict how data moves but also reflect the system's current state, offering dynamic insights into live operations. Imagine a logistics company monitoring shipments. A real-time dashboard could show the movement of tracking data from warehouses to customer notifications, highlighting delays or errors in the process as they occur. Such tools empower developers and stakeholders alike to address issues proactively, maintain system health, and ensure smooth operations.

Understanding data transformations is another critical element of data flow visualization. Rarely does data remain static as it moves through a system. It is filtered, aggregated, enriched, or reformatted depending on its purpose. Visualizing these transformations provides insight into how raw data evolves into actionable information. Consider, for example, a recommendation engine for an e-commerce platform. It might start with raw user click data, process it into behavioral patterns, and finally generate personalized product suggestions. By visualizing these stages, developers can better understand the algorithms at work, identify inefficiencies, and ensure the integrity of the final output.

Collaboration benefits immensely from clear data flow visualizations. In complex projects, team members often work on different parts of the system, from front-end interfaces to back-end services. A well-crafted visualization serves as a common language, bridging gaps in understanding and aligning efforts toward shared goals. For instance, when integrating a new feature, the front-end team and back-end team can reference the same diagram to ensure data flows seamlessly from the user interface to the database and back. This shared understanding reduces miscommunication and fosters a more cohesive development process.

Security is another area where data flow visualization proves invaluable. By mapping the pathways of sensitive data, such as personal information or financial transactions, developers can identify potential vulnerabilities. For instance, if a diagram reveals that unencrypted data passes through an insecure network segment, it becomes clear where protective measures like encryption or secure channels are necessary. Visualizations can also highlight areas where access controls or logging mechanisms are insufficient, ensuring compliance with regulations and safeguarding against breaches.

Historical data flows, though often overlooked, can also play a crucial role in understanding system behavior. Visualizing how data has moved through a system over time provides insights into trends, anomalies, and changes in usage patterns. For example, an analytics platform might visualize the flow of user event data during a product launch, revealing unexpected spikes in traffic or bottlenecks in processing pipelines. This retrospective view not only aids in post-mortem analysis but also informs future design decisions, helping developers anticipate and prepare for similar scenarios.

Despite its advantages, effective data flow visualization requires careful planning and execution. Overcomplicating diagrams or tools can lead to confusion rather than clarity. A balance must be struck between detail and simplicity, ensuring that the visualization communicates the necessary information without overwhelming the viewer. Additionally, visualizations should remain up to date. As systems evolve, outdated diagrams lose their relevance and can even mislead developers, causing errors or inefficiencies. Regularly revisiting and revising these visualizations ensures their ongoing utility.

Understanding Code Dependencies

Code dependencies are the invisible threads that weave through any software system, binding its components together. Whether explicit or implicit, these dependencies shape how systems are built, maintained, and scaled. Understanding them is not merely a technical exercise but a cornerstone of creating resilient, efficient, and maintainable software. Dependencies can empower systems to function seamlessly, but they can also become liabilities if left unchecked, introducing fragility that makes even minor changes a daunting challenge.

At its core, a dependency exists whenever a piece of code relies on another to function. This could be as simple as one function calling another or as complex as an application relying on multiple third-party libraries, frameworks, or external services. Dependencies are natural and often essential. No system exists in isolation, and the ability to leverage existing code—whether through libraries or internal modules—accelerates development and avoids reinventing the wheel. However, the degree to which code depends on external or internal components determines its flexibility and long-term viability.

Understanding internal dependencies begins with examining how modules, functions, and classes interact within a codebase. When one module relies heavily on the implementation details of another, it creates tight coupling. Tight coupling can make changes to one module ripple through the system, causing unintended side effects. For instance, consider a scenario where a payment processing module directly accesses the database schema of an order management system. If the database schema changes, the payment module could break, even though its core functionality remains unrelated to the schema modification. Recognizing these tightly bound relationships is the first step in identifying areas where systems can be decoupled for improved stability.

Loose coupling, on the other hand, is a hallmark of robust systems. It ensures that components interact through well-defined interfaces rather than direct access to internal details. By defining clear contracts for communication between modules, developers can isolate changes to specific parts of the system. For example, instead of allowing a front-end application to directly query a database, an API layer can serve as the intermediary. This abstraction not only simplifies testing and debugging but also allows each layer to evolve independently.

External dependencies introduce another layer of complexity. These include third-party libraries, APIs, frameworks, or services that a system relies on to function. While external dependencies can save development time and provide access to sophisticated tools, they also introduce risk. Changes or disruptions in an external dependency can cascade into your system. For example, a sudden update to a widely used library might deprecate key functionality or introduce breaking changes, leaving your application scrambling to adapt. Similarly, relying on an external API for critical functionality means your system is vulnerable to downtime or performance issues outside your control.

Mitigating the risks of external dependencies requires vigilance and proactive management. One effective strategy is to encapsulate external dependencies within wrapper functions or modules. By creating an abstraction layer, you shield the rest of your code from changes in the dependency's interface. For instance, if your application relies on a third-party email service, creating a dedicated email utility module that interacts with the service allows you to modify or replace the dependency with minimal disruption to your codebase.

Another important consideration is dependency versioning. Many developers have experienced the frustration of "dependency hell," where conflicts arise because different parts of a system rely on incompatible versions of the same library. Understanding how versioning affects your project—and diligently managing dependencies with tools like package managers—can prevent these conflicts. Locking versions, using semantic versioning principles, and staying informed about updates are critical practices for maintaining stability.

Implicit dependencies are often more insidious than explicit ones. They arise when code indirectly relies on behaviors or assumptions that are not immediately obvious. For example, a function might depend on a global variable being set to a specific value, or a module might assume that another has already loaded a particular resource. These hidden dependencies can lead to subtle bugs that are difficult to trace and fix.

Detecting implicit dependencies requires a combination of thorough documentation, code reviews, and systematic testing.

Cyclic dependencies represent a particularly challenging form of dependency. They occur when two or more components directly or indirectly depend on each other, creating a circular chain. This can lead to issues such as infinite loops, deadlocks, or difficulties in determining initialization order. For instance, if a logging module depends on a configuration module that in turn depends on the logging module for error reporting, a cycle is created. Breaking these cycles often requires rethinking the architecture, such as introducing a mediator component or refactoring dependencies into more granular units.

Dependency graphs are a powerful tool for visualizing and understanding the relationships within a system. By mapping out how components depend on one another, these graphs can reveal hidden complexities, bottlenecks, or areas of tight coupling. For example, a dependency graph might show that a single utility module is used across multiple parts of a system. While this reuse might initially seem efficient, it also means that changes to this module have the potential to impact the entire codebase. Identifying such critical points allows developers to take preventive measures, such as adding tests or creating isolated interfaces.

Dependency injection is another technique that promotes flexibility and reduces coupling. Instead of hardcoding dependencies within a module, they are passed in as parameters or configured externally. This approach makes it easier to replace or mock dependencies during testing, as well as to adapt the system to different environments. For example, a database module could be designed to accept a database connection as a dependency, allowing it to work with different database types or configurations without modification.

Testing plays a crucial role in managing dependencies. Unit tests ensure that individual components function correctly, while integration tests validate that dependencies between components work as expected. Mocking and stubbing are particularly useful for testing external dependencies, as they allow developers to simulate specific scenarios without relying on the actual external system. For instance, testing an application that relies on a payment gateway can involve creating a mock gateway to simulate success, failure, or timeout responses.

The goal of understanding and managing dependencies is not to eliminate them—dependencies are inevitable in any non-trivial system. Rather, it is to cultivate a codebase where dependencies are explicit, manageable, and resilient to change. By identifying points of fragility, decoupling tightly bound components, and embracing practices like dependency injection and thorough testing, developers can create systems that are both robust and adaptable. Dependencies, when understood and handled with care, become strengths rather than vulnerabilities, enabling systems to evolve gracefully over time.

Chapter 3: Debugging as Investigation

Reading Error Signatures

Errors are an inevitable part of software development, and reading error signatures is a skill that can distinguish an efficient developer from a frustrated one. Error signatures are not just cryptic messages; they are the breadcrumbs left behind by the system to guide you toward understanding what went wrong. They hold the potential to reveal bugs, uncover misconfigurations, or highlight deeper architectural issues. Mastering the interpretation of these signatures requires patience, logical thinking, and an ability to decipher patterns within chaos.

Every error tells a story. Whether it's a syntax error, a runtime exception, or a compilation failure, the message contains clues about the issue's origin. Consider an example: a developer runs their code and encounters an error that reads, "NullReferenceException: Object reference not set to an instance of an object." At first glance, this might seem like a generic and unhelpful message. However, by dissecting it, the developer can uncover vital information. It indicates that the program attempted to access an object that hasn't been properly initialized. With this knowledge, the focus narrows to specific areas of the code where objects are created and used, turning a seemingly vague message into a clear starting point for debugging.

The context in which an error occurs is just as important as the error message itself. Typically, error signatures are accompanied by stack traces, which provide a detailed map of the sequence of function calls leading up to the error. A stack trace is like a photograph of the system at the moment it failed, capturing the state of execution. For example, if a developer sees a stack trace showing a series of method calls within a payment processing service, they know exactly which part of the application to investigate. Each line in the stack trace represents a step in the chain of events, and understanding this hierarchy makes it possible to pinpoint the origin of the problem.

However, not all error signatures are straightforward. Sometimes, the problem lies far from where the error manifests. This is particularly true in distributed systems, where multiple services and components interact. Imagine an online marketplace application where a user encounters an error while placing an order. The error message might suggest an issue with the checkout service, but the root cause could reside in the inventory service failing to update stock levels. In such cases, tracing the flow of data and examining logs across different services becomes essential. Error signatures in distributed systems often require a holistic approach, piecing together information from multiple sources to form a complete picture.

Patterns in error signatures often repeat themselves, and recognizing these patterns can significantly speed up debugging. For instance, a "FileNotFoundException" typically points to an issue with file paths or permissions. A "Segmentation Fault" in a low-level language like C often indicates an attempt to access memory incorrectly. Over time, developers build a mental library of such patterns, enabling them to diagnose issues more quickly. This familiarity isn't limited to programming languages; it extends to specific frameworks and libraries. A seasoned developer working with a web framework might immediately recognize a database connection timeout error or an authentication failure signature, narrowing their investigation to the relevant configuration files or network settings.

Error signatures are not always generated by the code you write; they can also originate from dependencies. Libraries, frameworks, and APIs often throw errors when their contracts are violated. For example, if a library expects a JSON object and instead receives invalid syntax, it might throw a parsing error. In such cases, understanding how the dependency operates is crucial. Reading the documentation, exploring error codes provided by the dependency, or even diving into the source code of the library can offer insights. Dependencies often include their own error-handling mechanisms, and knowing how to work within those systems can make debugging far less daunting.

Silent failures, where an error does not produce a signature, are among the most challenging issues to address. These situations often arise when the system fails gracefully but not correctly, hiding the symptoms of a deeper problem. For example, a background task may fail silently without logging an error, leading to incomplete processes or missing data. Detecting and resolving silent failures often requires proactive measures, such as implementing logging at critical points in the code, adding assertions to validate assumptions, or setting up monitoring tools to catch anomalies during runtime.

A common mistake when dealing with error signatures is jumping to conclusions based on the message alone. Errors can be misleading, especially if they cascade from an earlier issue. For instance, a syntax error might occur because a previous line of code introduced an unclosed string or bracket. Addressing the immediate error without examining its context can lead to a cycle of fixing symptoms rather than solving the root cause. A systematic approach, starting from the first point of failure and moving outward, ensures that the underlying issue is resolved.

Collaborating with logs and diagnostic tools can amplify the effectiveness of reading error signatures. Logs provide a chronological record of events leading up to the error, offering additional context that error messages alone cannot. For example, if a server crashes with a "SocketException" due to too many open connections, the logs might reveal a pattern of connections not being properly closed in a specific workflow. Diagnostic tools, such as profilers or debuggers, go even further by allowing developers to inspect the state of variables, memory usage, and performance metrics at the time of failure. These tools turn error signatures into actionable insights.

Language and framework-specific nuances also play a role in interpreting error signatures. Some languages, like Python, provide verbose and human-readable error messages, making it easier to diagnose issues. Others, like C++, may produce cryptic output that requires deeper knowledge of the language internals. Similarly, some frameworks include error codes and detailed documentation to accompany their error messages, while others might leave developers to infer the meaning. Familiarity with the tools and technologies in use is critical for making sense of their error-handling behavior.

The ultimate goal of reading error signatures is not merely to fix bugs but to prevent them from recurring. Once an error is resolved, it's important to identify why it happened and what safeguards can be implemented to avoid similar issues in the future. This might involve adding additional error handling, improving input validation, or restructuring fragile parts of the codebase. Each error signature is an opportunity to learn, refine, and strengthen the system, transforming failure into a stepping stone for progress.

Errors are not obstacles; they are guides. The ability to read and interpret their signatures transforms them from frustrating interruptions into valuable insights. By approaching them with curiosity, patience, and a systematic mindset, developers can unlock the stories they tell, ensuring that the systems they build become more robust, reliable, and resilient with every challenge they overcome.

Tracing System Behavior

System behavior is the living pulse of software, a constant interplay of inputs, operations, and outputs that defines how applications respond to the world around them. Tracing this behavior is akin to unearthing a trail left by a traveler; it's about following the footsteps of processes, identifying their interactions, and uncovering hidden patterns. This skill is essential for understanding how a system operates under various circumstances, diagnosing issues, and ensuring its alignment with intended functionality. It's not just about observing what happens, but deciphering why it happens and how those occurrences influence the system as a whole.

Systems rarely function in isolation. They are dynamic entities, continuously interacting with users, external services, and their internal components. Tracing system behavior begins with capturing the journey of these interactions. Consider a user submitting a request to an online shopping platform. The journey might start with a click on a "Buy Now" button, followed by the request being sent to a server, processed for inventory verification, and finalized with a confirmation of purchase. Each step in this sequence is a node in the system's behavior, and tracing it provides a lens into what occurs at every stage, from the user's action to the system's response.

Logs are often the starting point for this exploration. Every significant event in a system can be recorded in logs, providing a chronological history of its actions. For example, a log entry might detail that a request was received at a particular time, processed by a specific service, and then forwarded to another service. These records become invaluable when something goes wrong, offering timestamps, error codes, or even contextual data that can narrow down the investigation. A developer tracing a failed transaction in a banking system might find that the logs reveal an authentication error, giving immediate direction to focus on the login process rather than the transaction itself.

Tracing system behavior, however, requires more than passive observation. It involves actively following the flow of data and operations through the system. Tools like distributed tracing platforms allow developers to visualize how requests propagate across components in complex architectures. Imagine a microservices-based application where a user request passes through multiple services for processing. Distributed tracing can reveal how long each service took to respond, where delays occurred, or whether any service failed altogether. This level of insight transforms an opaque system into one where every interaction is visible and measurable.

The temporal nature of system behavior is crucial to understanding its dynamics. Systems are not static; they evolve over time, and their performance can vary depending on the circumstances. For instance, a web application might handle traffic smoothly during normal hours but struggle during peak usage. Tracing system behavior in such scenarios involves monitoring how workloads change, how resources are allocated, and where bottlenecks might emerge. A sudden spike in database query times could indicate that a particular query is inefficient under heavy load, requiring optimization to prevent cascading performance issues.

Tracing also uncovers dependencies within the system, highlighting how components rely on one another. Dependencies are not inherently problematic, but they can create vulnerabilities if not managed properly. For instance, a service that depends on an external API for data might encounter failures if the API experiences downtime. Tracing the system's behavior during such an event reveals how the failure propagates and whether fallback mechanisms or retries function as intended. This understanding informs decisions about improving resilience, such as implementing caching or introducing redundancy.

In modern architectures, asynchronous operations add another layer of complexity to tracing. Operations that occur out of sync with the main request flow—such as background jobs, message queues, or scheduled tasks—can have a profound impact on system behavior. Consider an e-commerce platform that processes order payments asynchronously. Tracing the behavior of the payment service involves not only examining when the payment request was initiated but also monitoring how it was queued, processed, and confirmed. Asynchronous activities can introduce latency or failures that are difficult to detect without a deliberate tracing strategy.

Debugging is often where tracing system behavior becomes most critical. When something breaks, understanding the sequence of events leading to the failure is essential. A misconfiguration in a deployment, for example, might cause a service to crash, but the root cause could reside in an earlier step, such as an update to a dependent library. By retracing the system's actions, developers can reconstruct the path to failure, identifying the exact point where things went awry. This process relies on a combination of intuition, logical reasoning, and a detailed understanding of the system's inner workings.

Metrics complement tracing by providing quantitative data on system performance. While tracing shows the "how" and "why" of system behavior, metrics reveal trends and anomalies. For instance, a sudden increase in memory usage might signal a memory leak, which tracing can then investigate further. Together, metrics and tracing provide a comprehensive view of the system, enabling both proactive monitoring and reactive debugging.

Tracing system behavior also plays a role in optimizing performance. By following the flow of requests, developers can identify inefficiencies, such as redundant operations or slow components. Imagine a search engine feature where user queries are processed by multiple filters before returning results. Tracing might reveal that one filter consistently takes longer than others, suggesting an opportunity for optimization. Such insights not only improve response times but also enhance the user experience by making the system more efficient and reliable.

Security concerns often emerge during the process of tracing. Malicious activity, such as unauthorized access or data breaches, can leave subtle traces within a system. For example, an unusually high number of failed login attempts might indicate a brute force attack in progress. Tracing system behavior in this context allows developers to detect and respond to threats before they escalate. Additionally, understanding how data flows through the system helps ensure compliance with privacy regulations, as it reveals where sensitive information is stored, processed, or transmitted.

The act of tracing is not limited to addressing issues; it is a continuous process that informs the evolution of the system. As new features are added or old ones are retired, tracing ensures that the system remains cohesive and functional. It bridges the gap between design and execution, providing a real-time understanding of how individual components contribute to the whole. This ongoing practice fosters a culture of transparency and accountability, where every aspect of the system is open to scrutiny and improvement.

System behavior is the heartbeat of software, and tracing it is an exercise in discovery. It reveals not only how the system functions but also how it falters and adapts. By following the trails of requests, examining dependencies, and interpreting anomalies, developers gain the insight needed to build systems that are not only functional but also resilient, scalable, and secure. Tracing is more than a technical skill; it is a way of perceiving the system as a living, breathing entity, one whose behavior is as critical as its code.

Root Cause Analysis

Problems in a system rarely emerge in isolation. They are symptoms of deeper issues, often hidden beneath layers of complexity. Root cause analysis is the practice of peeling back these layers to identify the underlying source of a problem, rather than simply addressing its surface manifestations. It's a disciplined, methodical approach that transforms chaotic situations into opportunities for learning and improvement. By understanding the true cause, not only can the immediate issue be resolved, but steps can be taken to prevent its recurrence, making this an essential process for maintaining robust and resilient systems.

The first step in any root cause analysis is recognizing that problems often present themselves through symptoms. A system failure might manifest as a server crash, a delayed response, or corrupted data, but these are rarely the problem themselves. They are indicators, much like a fever signals an underlying illness. For example, an application might experience sporadic downtime. While a quick fix might involve rebooting the server to restore functionality, the real question is why the downtime occurred in the first place. Was it due to a memory leak, an unhandled exception, or perhaps an external dependency failing? Without identifying the root cause, the issue is likely to reappear, potentially with even greater consequences.

Understanding the chain of events leading to a problem lies at the heart of root cause analysis. Often, systems fail because of a sequence of seemingly minor issues that converge at a critical point. Imagine a distributed application where a database query starts taking longer than expected. Initially, the delay goes unnoticed, but as traffic increases, the slow query begins to saturate the database connection pool.

Eventually, the application becomes unresponsive. The immediate symptom might be identified as a timeout error, but the root cause could be traced back to poor query optimization or insufficient indexing. By reconstructing the timeline of events, the interdependencies and weak points within the system are revealed.

Asking the right questions is a fundamental skill in this process. One effective technique is the "Five Whys" method, which involves repeatedly asking "why" to move beyond superficial explanations. For instance, consider a scenario where a software deployment fails. Why did it fail? Perhaps a configuration file was missing. Why was the file missing? Because it wasn't included in the deployment package. Why wasn't it included? Because the build script didn't account for it. Why didn't the script account for it? Because the configuration file was added after the script was written, and no one updated the script. Each answer peels back another layer, bringing the root cause into focus. This iterative process not only uncovers the issue but also highlights systemic gaps, such as weaknesses in documentation or testing practices.

Data and evidence play a critical role in root cause analysis. Without concrete information, the process risks devolving into speculation. Logs, metrics, and traces provide a factual basis for investigation, offering snapshots of the system's behavior at the time of failure. For example, logs might reveal that a spike in error rates coincided with a specific API call, pointing to a problematic feature or integration. Metrics, such as CPU usage or memory consumption, can help identify resource constraints, while traces map the flow of requests through the system, highlighting bottlenecks or failures. By anchoring the analysis in evidence, developers can avoid chasing false leads and focus on actionable insights.

Collaboration is another essential aspect of effective root cause analysis. Complex systems often involve multiple teams, each responsible for different components. When a problem arises, it's rarely confined to a single area. A failure in one service might cascade into others, creating a chain reaction. Bringing together representatives from all relevant teams fosters a holistic understanding of the system and ensures that no perspective is overlooked. For instance, a network issue causing intermittent connectivity might initially seem unrelated to a slow-loading application. However, by combining insights from the network and application teams, the connection between the two can be uncovered, leading to a comprehensive solution.

Bias can be a significant obstacle during root cause analysis. It's easy to jump to conclusions, especially when similar issues have been encountered before. A developer might assume that a database timeout is due to high traffic because that was the cause in a previous incident. However, this assumption can blind them to other possibilities, such as a misconfigured connection pool or a network latency issue. Remaining objective and questioning assumptions is critical to avoiding these pitfalls. Each problem is unique, and while patterns can be useful, they should not dictate the investigation.

Once the root cause is identified, the next step is determining how to address it. Immediate remediation might involve fixing the specific issue, but long-term prevention requires addressing the systemic factors that allowed the problem to occur. For instance, if a bug in a critical piece of code caused a production outage, fixing the bug is only part of the solution. Implementing additional code reviews, automated testing, or monitoring could prevent similar issues from slipping through in the future. Root cause analysis doesn't end with solving the problem; it's about improving the system as a whole.

Documenting the findings is just as important as resolving the issue. A detailed record of the root cause, the steps taken to identify it, and the measures implemented to prevent recurrence serves as a valuable resource for the future. It ensures that knowledge is shared across the team and prevents the same mistakes from being made again. For example, if an incident report reveals that a specific API endpoint caused a bottleneck, future developers working on that endpoint can learn from past experiences and avoid repeating them. Documentation also provides transparency, demonstrating to stakeholders that the issue was thoroughly investigated and resolved.

The value of root cause analysis extends beyond individual incidents. Over time, patterns begin to emerge, revealing systemic issues that might otherwise go unnoticed. Perhaps multiple incidents trace back to inadequate testing environments or miscommunication between teams. By addressing these larger trends, organizations can improve not only their systems but also their processes, culture, and collaboration. Root cause analysis becomes a tool for continuous improvement, ensuring that each failure strengthens the system rather than weakening it.

At its essence, root cause analysis is about understanding. It's about digging below the surface to uncover the mechanisms and decisions that led to failure. It's about recognizing that problems are not isolated events but part of a larger context. With each analysis, systems become more resilient, teams grow more skilled, and organizations move closer to building software that not only works but thrives in the face of complexity. It is a practice of curiosity, discipline, and commitment, transforming failure into a foundation for success.

Performance Bottleneck Detection

Performance bottlenecks are the invisible culprits that can grind even the most well-designed systems to a halt. They are the points where the flow of data, processing, or communication slows down, creating inefficiencies that ripple across the entire system. Detecting such bottlenecks is not purely about identifying slow components but understanding why they are slow, when those slowdowns occur, and how they impact the broader architecture. This process is both an art and a science, requiring methodical investigation, precise tools, and a deep understanding of the system's behavior under various conditions.

Bottlenecks often reveal themselves under stress. A system might perform flawlessly with a handful of users but falter under the load of thousands. This illustrates how bottlenecks are not always visible during development or testing phases but emerge when the system operates in real-world environments. Imagine a video streaming platform that runs seamlessly during regular hours but struggles during the release of a highly anticipated series. The sudden influx of users could overwhelm the database handling user sessions, causing delays or failures in login processes. The challenge lies in detecting the exact component that becomes the limiting factor under such peak conditions.

A logical starting point is often to measure the system's performance and identify anomalies. Metrics such as response time, throughput, and resource utilization provide a snapshot of how the system behaves. For instance, if response times spike while CPU usage remains low, it might suggest that the bottleneck lies in an I/O operation, such as reading from a disk or waiting for an external API response. On the other hand, if CPU usage is consistently maxed out, it could point to inefficient algorithms, excessive computation, or resource contention. These metrics act as breadcrumbs, guiding developers toward the sections of the system that warrant deeper scrutiny.

Logs also play a pivotal role in bottleneck detection. Well-structured logs capture the sequence and duration of operations, offering a detailed timeline of events. For example, in a web application, logs might show that database queries are taking longer than expected, while application logic executes within normal parameters. This insight narrows the focus to the database layer, allowing developers to investigate whether the issue stems from poorly optimized queries, missing indexes, or contention caused by concurrent requests. Without such detailed records, the process of identifying bottlenecks can become a frustrating exercise in guesswork.

Profiling tools provide another layer of granularity by capturing real-time insights into how resources are being utilized. These tools reveal which functions, methods, or processes are consuming the most time or resources. Imagine a scenario where a batch processing job takes hours to complete. A profiler might uncover that a single function—responsible for sorting data—is consuming 80% of the execution time. Further investigation could reveal that the function uses an inefficient algorithm that performs poorly with large datasets. This level of detail allows developers to make targeted optimizations, often with significant performance gains.

In many cases, bottlenecks are not isolated to a single component but arise from the interactions between multiple parts of the system. Consider a microservices architecture where a user request involves calls to several services. If one service has a slower response time, it can create a cascading effect, delaying the entire operation. Distributed tracing tools are invaluable in such scenarios, as they map the flow of requests across services, highlighting where delays occur. For example, tracing might reveal that a payment gateway service consistently takes longer to respond during high traffic, pointing to issues like network latency, inadequate scaling, or overloaded dependencies.

Concurrency adds another layer of complexity to bottleneck detection. Systems designed to handle multiple users or processes simultaneously can encounter issues like thread contention, deadlocks, or race conditions. A classic example is a web server that spawns threads to handle incoming requests. If the number of threads exceeds the system's capacity, contention for shared resources like memory or database connections can degrade performance. Monitoring tools that track thread activity, lock contention, or queue lengths can uncover these issues, enabling developers to balance concurrency levels and resource allocation.

External dependencies often exacerbate performance bottlenecks. APIs, third-party services, or external databases introduce factors beyond the system's direct control. For instance, a payment processing API might experience delays, causing transactions to time out. While the root cause lies outside the system, it is the system's responsibility to handle such scenarios gracefully. Timeout settings, retries, or fallback mechanisms can mitigate the impact, but detecting these bottlenecks still requires careful monitoring of external calls and their response times.

Environmental factors also play a role in bottleneck detection. The same system might perform differently across environments due to variations in hardware, network configurations, or resource limits. A load-balanced application deployed across multiple servers might encounter issues if one server has a misconfigured setting, creating an uneven distribution of traffic. Stress testing in environments that closely replicate production conditions can help uncover such discrepancies before they affect end users. Tools that simulate real-world traffic patterns or inject failures into the system can provide insights into how it behaves under stress, revealing hidden bottlenecks.

Once a bottleneck is detected, the next step is to analyze its root cause and evaluate potential solutions. This often involves iterating through hypotheses, testing changes, and measuring their impact. For example, if a database query is identified as a bottleneck, adding an index might improve performance, but only if the query pattern aligns with the index. Similarly, scaling a service horizontally might alleviate performance issues, but only if the bottleneck is related to capacity rather than inefficiencies in the code. This iterative process requires a combination of technical expertise, experimentation, and a willingness to question assumptions.

Communication is critical during bottleneck detection, especially in collaborative environments. Developers, operations teams, and other stakeholders must share their insights and findings to build a comprehensive understanding of the issue. For example, while developers might focus on optimizing code, operations teams might identify network-related factors that contribute to delays. Combining these perspectives ensures a holistic approach, preventing solutions that address symptoms but leave underlying issues unresolved.

The ultimate goal of bottleneck detection is not just to resolve immediate performance issues but to build a system that can adapt to future demands. Each bottleneck represents an opportunity to learn more about the system, refine its design, and improve its resilience. By continuously monitoring, analyzing, and addressing bottlenecks, teams can ensure that their systems remain responsive, scalable, and efficient, even as requirements and workloads evolve. This proactive mindset transforms bottleneck detection from a reactive process into an integral part of system development and maintenance, enabling software to thrive in the face of growing complexity.

Debugging Mindset and Methodology

Debugging is rarely a straightforward process. It's a combination of science and intuition, logic and creativity, patience and persistence. A bug, no matter how small or obscure, can disrupt the entire flow of a system, making it critical to approach debugging with the right mindset and methodology. Without a structured approach, the process can quickly devolve into frustration and wasted time, but with the right perspective and techniques, debugging transforms into an opportunity to deepen your understanding of the system and improve its integrity.

The first step in developing a debugging mindset is to embrace the inevitability of bugs. No system is perfect, and no developer is infallible. Bugs are not failures in the traditional sense; they are natural byproducts of complexity. This realization reframes debugging as a challenge to be solved rather than a problem to be avoided. Accepting this reality helps you stay calm and focused when issues arise. Panic or frustration clouds judgment, leading to hasty decisions or missed details. Approaching debugging with curiosity and an open mind turns the process into an investigation, where every clue brings you closer to uncovering the truth.

A systematic methodology begins with defining the problem clearly. It's surprisingly easy to misinterpret the symptoms of a bug as the bug itself. For example, if a user reports that a web page is not loading, the root cause could be anything from a server outage to a JavaScript error on the client side. Starting with a vague description like "the page is broken" can lead to wasted effort chasing irrelevant leads. Instead, gather as much information as possible about the specific circumstances under which the issue occurs. Does it affect all users or only a subset? Does it happen consistently or intermittently? What actions trigger the bug? Answering these questions narrows the scope of the investigation, saving time and effort.

Once the problem is defined, the next step is to reproduce it. A bug that cannot be reproduced is nearly impossible to fix, as you have no way of verifying whether your changes address the issue. Reproducing the bug involves recreating the conditions under which it occurs, which might include specific inputs, configurations, or environments. For instance, an application might crash only when running on a particular operating system version or under heavy load. Reproducing these conditions in a controlled environment allows you to observe the bug directly, providing valuable insight into its nature.

As you work to identify the cause of the bug, resist the temptation to jump to conclusions. It's natural to rely on past experience or gut instincts, but debugging requires an objective approach. A common mistake is to assume that the problem lies in a specific part of the code without sufficient evidence. This can lead to tunnel vision, where you focus on one area while ignoring other possibilities. Instead, treat every hypothesis as a theory to be tested. Gather evidence through logs, error messages, or debugging tools to confirm or refute your assumptions. For example, if a database query is returning incorrect results, don't immediately assume the issue is with the query itself. It could be a problem with the data, the database configuration, or even the application logic that processes the query results.

Divide and conquer is a powerful strategy for isolating the root cause of a bug. Complex systems consist of multiple components, and tracing the flow of data or execution can reveal where things go wrong. Start by identifying the point at which the system behaves unexpectedly, and work backward or forward from there. For instance, if a web application fails to process a user's order, check whether the request reached the server, whether the server processed it correctly, and whether the response was sent back to the client. Each step in the sequence narrows the scope of the investigation, allowing you to focus on the specific component or interaction that is failing.

Debugging tools are invaluable allies in this process. Breakpoints, stack traces, and variable inspections allow you to step through the code and observe its behavior in real time. These tools help you verify whether the system is behaving as expected at each stage of execution. For example, setting a breakpoint in a function that calculates a user's discount can reveal whether the correct inputs are being passed and whether the calculation logic is working as intended. Similarly, examining a stack trace after an exception occurs provides a detailed record of the sequence of function calls leading up to the error, offering a roadmap for your investigation.

Collaboration can also play a significant role in debugging. Sometimes, a fresh perspective is all it takes to uncover a detail you may have overlooked. Explaining the problem to a colleague forces you to articulate your understanding of the issue, which can clarify your thinking or reveal inconsistencies. This technique, often called "rubber duck debugging," involves walking through the problem as if explaining it to a neutral party. Even without external input, the act of verbalizing your thought process can lead to breakthroughs.

Once the root cause is identified, the solution often becomes clear. However, it's essential to verify that your fix not only resolves the immediate issue but also prevents similar problems in the future. For example, if a function fails because it receives invalid input, adding input validation might address the bug while also improving the robustness of the system. Testing is crucial at this stage. Run the system under the same conditions that originally triggered the bug to ensure that it no longer occurs. Additionally, consider writing automated tests to catch similar issues before they reach production.

Reflecting on the debugging process is the final step. Every bug provides an opportunity to learn, whether it's about the system's intricacies, gaps in your understanding, or areas where the codebase could be improved. Documenting the bug, its root cause, and the solution ensures that the knowledge is preserved for future reference. It also helps identify patterns or recurring issues, which can inform broader changes to the system or development practices.

A debugging mindset is one of patience, curiosity, and discipline. It's about embracing the challenge, approaching the problem methodically, and viewing each bug as an opportunity to grow. With the right methodology, debugging becomes less of a chore and more of a rewarding process of discovery. The satisfaction of resolving a particularly stubborn bug is unmatched, not only because you've fixed the problem but because you've gained a deeper understanding of the system in the process. Debugging is not just about code; it's about perspective, persistence, and the pursuit of clarity.

Chapter 4: Code Evolution and Maintenance

Identifying Technical Debt
Technical debt often begins as a small compromise, a temporary decision made under pressing deadlines or resource constraints. It's the tradeoff between doing something quickly and doing it right, a shortcut taken with the intention of revisiting it later. Yet, as projects grow in complexity and priorities shift, this debt compounds, accumulating silently until it becomes an obstacle to progress. Identifying technical debt is the first step in addressing it, requiring an understanding of its subtle manifestations and its profound impact on system health, maintainability, and scalability.

The concept of technical debt can be deceptive because it doesn't always announce itself with immediate consequences. A piece of code written in haste might work perfectly well at first, delivering the desired functionality without apparent issues. Over time, however, as new features are added and the system evolves, that once-innocuous code becomes harder to maintain. It might be poorly documented, overly complex, or riddled with assumptions that no longer hold true. Developers tasked with modifying it find themselves spending hours deciphering its logic, introducing bugs as they attempt to adapt it to new requirements. The debt, initially invisible, has now become a drain on time and resources.

One of the most common indicators of technical debt is a decrease in development velocity. When every new feature or fix takes longer than expected because developers must work around existing code, it's often a sign that the system is burdened by debt. For example, consider a module in an e-commerce platform responsible for calculating shipping costs. If adding support for a new shipping partner requires weeks of effort due to entangled logic and hardcoded values, the module likely harbors significant debt. This slowdown is not merely an inconvenience; it reflects the hidden costs of past decisions, costs that continue to grow as the system ages.

Code complexity is another hallmark of technical debt. Overly complicated code, characterized by long functions, nested conditionals, or cryptic variable names, is difficult to understand and even more challenging to modify. Developers might avoid touching such code out of fear of breaking something, further exacerbating the problem. For instance, a legacy reporting system might include a single function spanning hundreds of lines, with calculations interspersed among database queries and formatting logic. Any attempt to refactor or extend this function risks introducing errors, making it a liability rather than an asset.

Inconsistent or missing documentation is a less obvious, but equally damaging, form of debt. Code that lacks comments or is poorly documented leaves future developers guessing at its purpose and intent. This issue becomes particularly acute when team members move on and institutional knowledge is lost. Imagine inheriting a codebase where critical business logic is embedded in a series of scripts with no accompanying explanation. Even if the code works, its opacity makes it difficult to trust or adapt, creating friction in the development process.

Testing gaps are another frequent source of technical debt. Tests are often the first casualty of tight deadlines, with teams prioritizing feature delivery over test coverage. While this might seem like a reasonable tradeoff in the short term, it leaves the system vulnerable to regressions and increases the risk of introducing bugs during future changes. A lack of automated tests forces developers to rely on manual testing or, worse, to skip testing altogether, turning even minor modifications into potential minefields. For instance, an application with no tests for its payment processing workflow risks critical errors that could compromise revenue or customer trust.

Outdated dependencies or technologies represent yet another form of technical debt. As libraries, frameworks, and tools evolve, older versions become unsupported, exposing the system to security vulnerabilities and compatibility issues. A web application built on an outdated framework might struggle to implement modern features or integrate with third-party services. Upgrading these dependencies often requires significant effort, particularly if the system was not designed with flexibility in mind. This form of debt is especially insidious because it accumulates gradually, often going unnoticed until it reaches a crisis point.

Team practices and processes can also contribute to technical debt. Poor version control practices, inconsistent coding standards, or a lack of code reviews create an environment where debt flourishes. For example, if developers frequently bypass the review process to expedite changes, the codebase might accumulate issues that only become apparent later. Similarly, if coding guidelines are not enforced, the system can become a patchwork of differing styles and approaches, making it harder to maintain.

Identifying technical debt requires a combination of observation, measurement, and dialogue. Developers often have an intuitive sense of where the debt lies, based on their experiences working with the system. Soliciting feedback from the team can reveal areas of the codebase that are particularly difficult to work with or prone to issues. Metrics such as code churn, where sections of code are repeatedly modified, or defect density, which tracks the number of bugs relative to the size of the code, provide quantitative indicators of debt. Tools that measure code quality, such as static analysis or cyclomatic complexity calculators, can highlight problem areas that warrant further investigation.

The consequences of technical debt extend beyond the technical domain. It affects team morale, as developers grow frustrated with the challenges of working on a debt-laden system. It also impacts stakeholders, who may experience delays, cost overruns, or reduced functionality. Left unchecked, technical debt can lead to a tipping point where the system becomes so fragile that even minor changes risk catastrophic failure. At this stage, the cost of addressing the debt far exceeds the cost of preventing it in the first place.

Recognizing technical debt is not about assigning blame but about acknowledging the tradeoffs inherent in software development. Every project involves constraints—time, budget, resources—that influence decision-making. Technical debt is the natural result of these constraints, but it does not have to be a permanent burden. By identifying and addressing debt early, teams can mitigate its impact and create systems that are not only functional but sustainable.

The process of identifying technical debt is an ongoing effort, one that requires vigilance and a commitment to quality. It involves examining not just the code but the practices, tools, and assumptions that shape the development process. Each instance of debt is an opportunity to learn and improve, to build systems that are not only efficient but resilient. The goal is not to eliminate debt entirely—a near-impossible task—but to manage it thoughtfully, ensuring that it serves the project rather than hindering it. Through this lens, technical debt becomes less of a liability and more of a guide, steering teams toward better decisions and stronger systems.

Recognizing Refactoring Opportunities

Codebases, like living organisms, evolve over time. What begins as a pristine and efficient structure eventually becomes tangled with new features, quick fixes, and compromises made under pressing deadlines. This natural progression often leads to code that is harder to maintain, less efficient, and increasingly fragile. Recognizing the need for refactoring—carefully improving the internal structure of code without altering its external behavior—is a critical skill for maintaining the long-term health of any system. The challenge lies in identifying opportunities for such improvements amidst the daily demands of software development.

One of the clearest indicators of the need for refactoring is code duplication. When similar logic appears in multiple places, it not only inflates the codebase but also creates a maintenance nightmare. If a change is required, every instance of the duplicated code must be updated, increasing the risk of inconsistencies and bugs. For example, imagine a system where the logic for calculating tax is repeated across several modules. If the tax rules change, developers must remember to update every occurrence of this logic, which can easily lead to errors if one instance is overlooked. Recognizing these patterns of duplication and consolidating them into a single, reusable function or module simplifies the code and reduces the likelihood of future mistakes.

Long and complex functions are another red flag signaling the need for refactoring. When a single function attempts to do too much, it becomes difficult to read, understand, and test. Such functions often emerge over time as developers add new functionality without considering the overall design. For instance, a function responsible for processing user registrations might start by validating input, then evolve to include database interactions, email notifications, and logging. While each addition might seem reasonable in isolation, the result is a sprawling function that no one fully understands. Breaking it into smaller, more focused functions not only improves readability but also makes the code easier to test and maintain.

Inconsistent naming conventions and unclear variable names are subtler signs of code that would benefit from refactoring. Code should communicate its intent clearly, allowing developers to understand what it does without extensive context or documentation. When variable names are vague or inconsistent, they create confusion and slow down development. For example, a variable named "temp" offers no indication of its purpose, while a name like "userAge" immediately conveys its intent. Renaming variables, functions, or classes to align with consistent naming conventions might seem like a minor change, but it can significantly improve the overall clarity and usability of the codebase.

Another common cue for refactoring is the presence of "magic numbers" or hardcoded values scattered throughout the code. These values, such as specific integers or strings, often represent important constants or configurations but are not immediately identifiable as such. Consider a scenario where a discount percentage of "10" is hardcoded into multiple parts of an application. If the discount policy changes, these values must be updated manually, which is error-prone and inefficient. Replacing magic numbers with named constants or configuration variables makes the code more flexible and easier to maintain.

Code with too many dependencies is a prime candidate for refactoring. When a class or function relies on an excessive number of other components, it becomes tightly coupled, making changes more difficult and increasing the risk of unintended side effects. For example, a service that directly invokes multiple database queries, external APIs, and utility functions is less adaptable to changes in any of these dependencies. By introducing abstraction layers or dependency injection, the code can be decoupled, improving its modularity and testability.

Frequent bugs or regressions in specific parts of the codebase often indicate the need for refactoring. When developers repeatedly encounter issues in the same module, it suggests that the code is either too complex, poorly structured, or lacks sufficient safeguards. Consider a reporting tool that consistently produces errors when new data is added to the system. This pattern might point to brittle logic or improper handling of edge cases. Refactoring the code to address these weaknesses can reduce the frequency of bugs and make the system more robust.

Refactoring opportunities also become apparent during code reviews or collaborative discussions. When multiple developers struggle to understand a particular section of code or raise concerns about its readability and maintainability, it's a clear sign that changes are needed. Code that requires extensive explanation or context to comprehend is not only a barrier to collaboration but also a liability for future development. Simplifying such code through refactoring eliminates these roadblocks and fosters a more productive team dynamic.

The introduction of new features often reveals opportunities for refactoring as well. When adding functionality becomes disproportionately difficult due to existing code constraints, it's a sign that the current design is not flexible enough to accommodate growth. For instance, a notification system that was initially designed to handle only email notifications might become unwieldy when support for SMS and push notifications is added. Refactoring the system to use a more extensible design, such as a strategy pattern, allows for easier integration of future notification types.

Performance issues, while not always directly related to refactoring, can highlight areas of code that are overly complex or inefficient. A web application that experiences slow response times during peak usage might benefit from optimizing database queries, reducing redundant calculations, or simplifying data processing pipelines. While these changes are often performance-driven, they also improve the overall structure and quality of the code.

Recognizing refactoring opportunities requires a mindset of continuous improvement. It's not about making the code perfect but about making it better—more readable, maintainable, and adaptable. The decision to refactor should be driven by a clear understanding of the benefits it will bring, weighed against the time and effort required. Small, incremental improvements often have a cumulative effect, gradually transforming a codebase without disrupting ongoing development.

Refactoring is not just a technical exercise; it's an investment in the future of the system. By addressing issues early and iteratively, teams can prevent technical debt from accumulating to unmanageable levels. It's a proactive approach that ensures the codebase remains a solid foundation for growth, innovation, and sustainable development. Recognizing these opportunities is a skill that develops with experience and a commitment to quality, enabling developers to create systems that are not only functional but elegant and resilient.

Legacy Code Navigation

Legacy code is the kind of code that elicits a groan from developers, a tangle of outdated practices, cryptic logic, and forgotten intentions. It can feel like stepping into a dense forest without a map—every step revealing something unexpected, and often, unwelcome. Yet, legacy code is also the backbone of countless systems, powering critical applications and processes. Navigating it is not just an exercise in survival but a test of a developer's skill, patience, and creativity. Understanding how to approach it effectively is essential for maintaining, improving, and extending the functionality of these systems without introducing new issues.

One of the first challenges in dealing with legacy code is understanding what you're looking at. Legacy code rarely comes with adequate documentation, with comments either missing entirely or woefully outdated. The code itself may be written in a style that's unfamiliar, using patterns, libraries, or even programming languages that have long since fallen out of favor. It's tempting to dive in and start making changes, but doing so without fully grasping the context is a recipe for disaster. Before touching anything, take the time to observe. Read through the code to identify its structure, purpose, and flow. Look for entry points—functions or methods that seem to act as the starting place for a particular process. While this can feel tedious, it's the equivalent of surveying a landscape before beginning construction. Without this foundational understanding, you risk knocking down the wrong walls.

One of the most effective tools for understanding legacy code is the debugger. By stepping through the code as it runs, you can see its behavior in real time, following the flow of execution and observing the state of variables. This can reveal dependencies, side effects, and hidden logic that might not be immediately apparent from reading the code alone. For example, a function that calculates discounts might seem straightforward until you notice, through debugging, that it makes a silent call to another function that modifies the database. Such discoveries are critical for understanding how the code actually works versus how it appears to work.

Logs are another invaluable resource. Well-placed logging statements can provide insight into how the system behaves in different scenarios. If the legacy system already includes logging, examine the logs to piece together the sequence of events leading to a particular outcome. If logging is sparse or nonexistent, consider adding temporary log statements at key points in the code to gain visibility. For instance, if you're investigating why a scheduled task isn't running as expected, logging the inputs, outputs, and execution times of the relevant functions can help pinpoint the issue.

Testing, or the lack thereof, is a significant obstacle when dealing with legacy code. Many legacy systems were built without automated tests, leaving you without a safety net when making changes. Before modifying anything, consider creating a suite of tests to establish a baseline for the code's current behavior. These tests don't have to be exhaustive; even a handful of basic tests can provide reassurance that your changes haven't broken existing functionality. For example, if you're tasked with updating a payment processing system, writing tests to confirm that payments are still processed correctly under various scenarios can prevent costly errors.

As you navigate legacy code, you'll likely encounter areas that are unnecessarily complex. Functions with dozens of parameters, classes with hundreds of methods, and deeply nested loops are all signs of code that has grown unwieldy over time. Resist the urge to refactor immediately. While it's tempting to clean up messy code, doing so without a thorough understanding of its purpose and dependencies can introduce new bugs. Instead, make a note of these areas and revisit them once you've established confidence in how the system operates. When you do refactor, aim for small, incremental changes that improve clarity without altering functionality.

Legacy systems often depend on outdated or poorly documented external libraries and frameworks. These dependencies can be a source of frustration, particularly if they behave unpredictably or lack modern features. Researching these libraries is crucial; understanding their quirks and limitations can save you hours of trial and error. Look for community forums, archived documentation, or even the library's source code to fill gaps in your knowledge. In some cases, you may need to consider replacing a dependency entirely, but this should be approached with caution. Replacing a library can have far-reaching consequences, particularly if it's deeply integrated into the system.

Collaboration plays a vital role in navigating legacy code. If you're working on a team, don't hesitate to ask for input from colleagues who have experience with the system. Even if no one on the team wrote the original code, someone may have investigated a similar issue or addressed a related bug in the past. Pair programming can be particularly effective, as it allows two developers to combine their perspectives and problem-solving skills. Explaining your understanding of the code to someone else often clarifies your own thinking and highlights gaps in your knowledge.

Patience is perhaps the most important quality when working with legacy code. It's easy to become frustrated with unclear logic, outdated practices, or unexpected behaviors. However, approaching the code with an open mind and a sense of curiosity can transform the experience. Every line of legacy code tells a story, revealing decisions made by developers who were likely working under constraints you may never fully understand. By respecting the code and the context in which it was written, you can approach your work with the humility and care it requires.

Finally, as you make changes to legacy code, document your findings and decisions. Add comments to clarify the purpose of particularly opaque sections, update any existing documentation, and share your insights with the team. Legacy code doesn't have to remain mysterious and inaccessible; by contributing to its understanding, you make it easier for the next developer who encounters it. Over time, these incremental improvements can transform a difficult and intimidating codebase into one that is manageable and even welcoming.

Navigating legacy code is a challenge, but it's also an opportunity. It forces you to think critically, adapt to unfamiliar contexts, and sharpen your technical skills. More than that, it's a chance to breathe new life into a system that has served its purpose over the years and ensure that it continues to provide value in the future. By approaching legacy code with curiosity, discipline, and respect, you can turn what might seem like a burden into a rewarding and meaningful endeavor.

Change Impact Analysis

Every modification to a software system, no matter how minor it seems, ripples through its architecture. These ripples can be subtle, barely noticeable, or they can surface as dramatic, unintended consequences that destabilize the system. Change impact analysis is the practice of predicting those ripples before they unfold, ensuring that alterations to the codebase are deliberate, controlled, and safe. It isn't just about anticipating what will happen; it's about managing risk, maintaining system integrity, and making well-informed decisions.

The first step in any effective impact analysis is understanding the change itself. Whether it's a bug fix, a feature enhancement, or a performance optimization, the scope of the modification must be clearly defined. Vague or incomplete requirements can lead to assumptions, and assumptions in software development are dangerous. For example, a request to "improve the loading speed of the dashboard" could encompass changes to database queries, front-end rendering, API calls, or even server configurations. Without a precise understanding of what the change involves, it's impossible to predict its impact accurately. This is why clear communication with stakeholders is critical. A shared understanding of the change's goals and constraints ensures that the analysis is grounded in reality.

Once the scope of the change is defined, the next step is to identify the areas of the system that will be directly affected. These are the points of direct interaction where code will be added, modified, or removed. For instance, if a change involves altering the calculation of discounts in an e-commerce application, the immediate focus would be the function responsible for that calculation. However, this is only the starting point. The true challenge lies in tracing the dependencies and connections that extend from these directly affected areas.

Dependencies are at the heart of impact analysis. Modern software systems are rarely linear or self-contained; they are intricate webs of interconnected modules, services, and components. A change to one part of the system inevitably affects others, sometimes in surprising ways. For example, modifying a function in a shared library might seem like a localized change, but if that library is used across multiple services, the impact can cascade throughout the system. Dependency maps, whether generated manually or with the help of tools, are invaluable for visualizing these connections. They provide a roadmap for tracing the flow of data, logic, and control, helping developers anticipate where issues might arise.

Historical data can also be a powerful ally in impact analysis. Bug reports, incident logs, and version histories offer a wealth of information about how similar changes have affected the system in the past. If a particular module has a history of regressions or compatibility issues, it warrants extra scrutiny. For instance, a payment gateway integration that has caused outages during previous updates should be treated with caution during future modifications. Learning from past experiences not only reduces risk but also builds a deeper understanding of the system's vulnerabilities and strengths.

Testing plays a central role in mitigating the risks identified during analysis. The goal of testing in this context isn't just to verify that the change works as intended but to ensure that it doesn't inadvertently break other parts of the system. This is where comprehensive test coverage becomes invaluable. Automated tests, particularly regression tests, provide a safety net, catching unintended side effects before they reach production. If the change involves a critical feature, such as user authentication or payment processing, additional stress tests and edge-case scenarios may be warranted. For example, if a change modifies how user sessions are handled, testing should include scenarios involving expired sessions, simultaneous logins, and unusual patterns of activity.

Stakeholder communication is another crucial element of impact analysis. Changes don't exist in isolation; they affect users, business processes, and other teams within the organization. Clear communication ensures that everyone understands the implications of the change and can prepare accordingly. For example, if a database schema update requires a brief downtime, stakeholders need to plan for the disruption, whether it's informing users or rescheduling dependent tasks. Transparency about the risks and trade-offs of the change builds trust and fosters collaboration, turning potential challenges into opportunities for alignment.

One of the most difficult aspects of impact analysis is acknowledging uncertainty. No matter how thorough the analysis, there will always be unknowns—areas of the system that are poorly understood, edge cases that escape detection, or external factors that come into play. This uncertainty is not a failure of the process but a reality of software development. The key is to account for it by building safeguards into the implementation plan. Rollback procedures, feature toggles, and incremental deployments are all strategies for managing the unexpected. For instance, deploying a change to a subset of users first allows you to monitor its impact in a controlled environment before rolling it out more broadly.

A change's impact isn't limited to the immediate aftermath of its implementation. Long-term effects, such as increased maintenance complexity or performance degradation, must also be considered. For example, adding a quick workaround for a bug might resolve the issue in the short term but create technical debt that complicates future development. Balancing immediate needs with long-term sustainability is a hallmark of effective impact analysis. It requires not only technical expertise but also a strategic perspective, one that weighs the benefits of the change against its potential costs over time.

Documentation is the final piece of the puzzle. Recording the findings of the analysis, the decisions made, and the rationale behind them creates a valuable resource for future reference. It ensures that the knowledge gained during the process isn't lost and provides a foundation for continuous improvement. For example, if a similar change needs to be made in the future, the documentation offers a starting point, saving time and reducing risk. It also fosters accountability, as decisions are grounded in a documented understanding of the system and its constraints.

Change impact analysis is both a science and an art. It combines logical reasoning with intuition, technical knowledge with strategic thinking. It's an exercise in humility, recognizing that no system is fully predictable, and an exercise in confidence, trusting in the process to guide you through uncertainty. By approaching changes with care, curiosity, and a deep commitment to quality, you not only preserve the integrity of the system but also build a culture of thoughtful, deliberate development. Every change becomes an opportunity to learn, improve, and strengthen the foundation on which the system stands.

Chapter 5: System Level Understanding

Component Interaction Patterns

Software systems are rarely composed of a single, monolithic block of code. Instead, they are built from multiple components, each with its own responsibilities, behaviors, and boundaries. These components interact with one another to achieve the system's overall objectives, forming intricate patterns of communication and collaboration. Understanding and designing these interaction patterns is crucial for creating systems that are efficient, maintainable, and scalable. The way components interact often determines whether a system is robust and flexible or brittle and difficult to extend.

One of the most fundamental aspects of component interaction is defining clear boundaries. Each component should have a well-defined purpose, encapsulating specific functionality and exposing only what is necessary to the outside world. This principle, often referred to as separation of concerns, ensures that components remain independent and can be developed, tested, and maintained in isolation. For example, in a web application, a user authentication component might handle tasks such as verifying credentials, managing sessions, and enforcing access control. By encapsulating these responsibilities, the component can interact with other parts of the system without exposing its internal workings. This separation minimizes the risk of unintended side effects when changes are made, as other components remain unaffected by the internal details.

The manner in which components communicate is another critical consideration. Synchronous communication, where one component waits for a response from another before proceeding, is straightforward and intuitive but can introduce coupling and bottlenecks. For instance, a payment processing system might require confirmation from a third-party service before completing a transaction. While this synchronous interaction ensures that the payment is verified in real time, it also ties the system's performance to the responsiveness of the external service. If the service experiences delays or downtime, the entire process is affected. Asynchronous communication offers an alternative, allowing components to send messages or requests without waiting for an immediate response. In the payment processing example, the system could queue the transaction for later verification, allowing other operations to continue uninterrupted. This decoupling improves resilience and scalability, though it requires careful handling of eventual consistency and error recovery.

Shared data is another common point of interaction between components. When multiple components access and modify the same data, it's essential to establish clear rules and mechanisms for managing these interactions. Without such rules, conflicts and inconsistencies can arise, leading to unpredictable behavior. Consider an e-commerce platform where an inventory management component and an order processing component both interact with the same database table to track stock levels. If these components update the table independently without coordination, it's possible for orders to be processed for items that are no longer in stock. Techniques such as locking, transactions, or event-driven architectures can mitigate these risks, ensuring that shared data remains consistent and reliable.

Event-driven interactions are particularly powerful in systems with loosely coupled components. Instead of directly invoking one another, components publish events that other components can subscribe to and react to as needed. This pattern enables a high degree of flexibility, as components can be added, removed, or replaced without affecting the overall system. For example, in a content management system, a "content published" event might trigger notifications, analytics updates, and caching refreshes, each handled by separate components. None of these components depend directly on the content publishing logic, allowing each to evolve independently. However, event-driven architectures also introduce complexity, as debugging and tracing the flow of events can become challenging in large systems.

Middleware and integration layers often play a central role in managing component interactions, particularly in systems composed of heterogeneous technologies. These layers act as intermediaries, standardizing communication protocols, translating data formats, and orchestrating workflows across disparate components. For instance, an enterprise resource planning (ERP) system might rely on middleware to connect its financial, inventory, and customer relationship management modules. By centralizing these interactions, the middleware reduces the complexity of direct connections between components, making the system easier to manage and extend. However, this approach comes with trade-offs, as the middleware itself can become a point of failure or a performance bottleneck if not designed carefully.

The design of component interaction patterns must also account for failure handling and recovery. No system is immune to failures, whether due to network outages, hardware malfunctions, or software bugs. When one component fails, it's essential to ensure that the rest of the system remains operational or degrades gracefully. Circuit breakers, retries, and fallback mechanisms are common strategies for managing failures in component interactions. For example, a recommendation engine in an e-commerce platform might rely on a machine learning model hosted on a separate server. If the server becomes unavailable, the recommendation engine could fall back to a simpler rule-based approach, ensuring that users still receive recommendations even if the system is operating in a degraded state.

Monitoring and observability are critical for maintaining healthy component interactions. Metrics, logs, and traces provide visibility into how components are communicating, allowing developers to identify and address performance bottlenecks, errors, or unexpected behaviors. For instance, a microservices architecture might include a centralized dashboard that aggregates data from individual services, showing response times, error rates, and throughput. This visibility enables proactive management of the system, ensuring that interactions between components remain efficient and reliable as the system evolves.

As systems grow in complexity, the importance of designing scalable interaction patterns becomes increasingly evident. Patterns that work well for a small number of components can become unwieldy as the number of interactions grows. For example, a tightly coupled architecture where every component communicates directly with every other component might suffice for a simple application but quickly leads to chaos as the system expands. By adopting patterns such as publish-subscribe, service registries, or message queues, developers can design systems that scale gracefully while maintaining clarity and manageability.

Component interaction patterns are the lifeblood of software systems, determining how individual pieces come together to form a cohesive whole. They reflect the delicate balance between independence and collaboration, simplicity and functionality, stability and adaptability. Thoughtful design in this area is not just a technical exercise but an investment in the system's future, ensuring that it remains robust, flexible, and capable of meeting evolving demands. By mastering these patterns, developers can create systems that not only work but thrive, delivering value today while laying a foundation for tomorrow.

Resource Management Insights

Efficient resource management is the backbone of any successful software system. Resources, whether they are CPU cycles, memory allocations, network bandwidth, or database connections, are finite by nature. Mismanagement not only leads to inefficiencies but can also cause severe disruptions, from performance degradation to system crashes. Understanding how to allocate, monitor, and optimize resources is critical for building systems that can scale and remain reliable under pressure.

One of the first challenges in resource management is understanding the demands of your application. Different workloads place varying levels of stress on system resources, and these demands often fluctuate over time. A high-traffic e-commerce website, for instance, will experience spikes during sales or holiday seasons, while a batch processing application may generate resource load in a predictable, cyclical pattern. Profiling the behavior of your application under real-world conditions is essential for identifying resource bottlenecks. Tools like performance profilers and monitoring dashboards can provide invaluable insights into how resources are consumed, helping developers pinpoint inefficiencies and plan for scalability.

Memory management is a cornerstone of resource optimization. Poor memory practices can lead to issues such as leaks, fragmentation, and exhaustion, each of which has the potential to cripple a system. For example, an application that fails to release unused memory will gradually consume all available RAM, leading to out-of-memory errors and system instability. Proper memory allocation and deallocation are critical, particularly in languages that don't handle garbage collection automatically. Even in languages with garbage collection, developers must be mindful of how objects are created, referenced, and discarded. For instance, retaining references to large data structures unnecessarily can prevent them from being cleaned up, resulting in excessive memory usage.

CPU utilization presents another layer of complexity in resource management. High CPU usage can indicate that the system is working efficiently, but it can also reveal bottlenecks or poorly optimized code. A background task that monopolizes the CPU with excessive computations, for example, might delay or block more critical operations. Profiling tools that measure CPU usage across threads and processes can uncover these inefficiencies, allowing developers to refactor code or redistribute workloads. Techniques such as parallel processing, multithreading, or offloading tasks to specialized hardware like GPUs can significantly improve performance when implemented thoughtfully.

Database connections and queries are frequently overlooked in discussions about resource management, yet they represent a major source of inefficiency in many systems. Databases are shared resources, and each connection consumes memory and processing power on the database server. Inefficient queries or an excessive number of connections can overwhelm the database, causing latency and timeouts. Connection pooling is a common solution, reusing a limited number of connections to serve multiple requests. Additionally, optimizing queries through indexing, avoiding unnecessary joins, and reducing data transfer can dramatically reduce the load on the database. For example, a reporting system that retrieves millions of rows of data for every request can be restructured to aggregate data at the database level, transferring only the summarized results to the application.

Network resources are another critical area, especially for distributed systems and applications that depend on external APIs or services. Latency, bandwidth limitations, and packet loss can all impact system performance. Efficient use of network resources involves minimizing the size and frequency of data transfers, caching frequently accessed data, and employing compression techniques. For instance, a web application that loads high-resolution images for every user request can significantly reduce bandwidth usage by implementing image compression and serving cached versions of images when appropriate. Additionally, load balancing across multiple servers or geographic regions can help distribute network traffic, ensuring that no single point of the system becomes a bottleneck.

Concurrency and parallelism introduce their own challenges in resource management. While they allow systems to perform multiple tasks simultaneously, they also increase the complexity of managing shared resources. Deadlocks, race conditions, and contention are common pitfalls when multiple threads or processes access the same resource. Imagine a payment processing system where two threads attempt to update the same user account balance simultaneously. Without proper locking or transaction mechanisms, the result could be inconsistent or incorrect data. Strategies like lock-free programming, optimistic concurrency control, or using thread-safe data structures can mitigate these risks while maintaining high performance.

Energy consumption is an often-overlooked aspect of resource management, particularly in resource-constrained environments such as mobile devices or embedded systems. Inefficient code that consumes excessive CPU cycles or keeps the network active unnecessarily drains battery life and reduces usability. Techniques such as optimizing algorithms, reducing wake-up calls for background processes, and leveraging low-power states of hardware can make a significant difference. For example, a mobile application that synchronizes data with a server every few seconds can be modified to synchronize only when changes occur, drastically reducing energy usage without compromising functionality.

Scalability is a key consideration in resource management, particularly for systems that must handle increasing workloads over time. Vertical scaling, or adding more resources to a single server, has its limits and often becomes cost-prohibitive. Horizontal scaling, which involves distributing the workload across multiple servers, is generally more flexible and cost-effective. For instance, a content delivery network (CDN) can serve static assets like images and videos from servers located closer to end users, reducing the load on the primary application servers and improving response times. However, scaling introduces additional challenges, such as maintaining consistency across distributed systems and managing resource allocation dynamically.

Monitoring and observability are indispensable for effective resource management. Real-time dashboards, alerting systems, and historical data analysis provide visibility into how resources are being utilized and help detect anomalies before they escalate into crises. For example, a sudden spike in database connections might indicate a bug in the application code or an unexpected surge in user activity. By setting thresholds and alerts for critical metrics, such as CPU usage, memory consumption, or network latency, teams can respond proactively to potential issues. Observability tools that provide detailed traces of requests and resource usage across components enable a deeper understanding of system behavior, facilitating targeted optimizations.

Effective resource management requires a balance between current needs and future growth. Overprovisioning resources might solve immediate performance issues but leads to waste and unnecessary costs. On the other hand, underprovisioning increases the risk of outages and degraded performance during peak usage. Planning for resource allocation should be an iterative process, informed by regular profiling, monitoring, and analysis. For example, a cloud-based system could use autoscaling to adjust resource allocation dynamically, ensuring that it meets demand without excessive overcommitment.

Resource management is as much about discipline and foresight as it is about technical skill.

Understanding the interplay between different types of resources and how they affect one another is a nuanced task that evolves with the system. By consistently measuring, analyzing, and optimizing resource usage, developers can create systems that are not only efficient and reliable but also prepared to adapt to future challenges. This commitment to resource stewardship ensures that the system delivers value to users while maintaining the flexibility to grow and evolve.

Scalability Indicators

Scalability is the ability of a system to handle increased load or demand without compromising performance, reliability, or functionality. It's not just about adding resources to meet growing needs but about designing systems that respond efficiently to that growth. Identifying when a system is approaching its limits requires careful observation and analysis of specific indicators. These signs often emerge gradually, and their detection can make the difference between a smooth scaling process and a rushed scramble to prevent system failure.

One of the earliest and most obvious indicators is a consistent increase in response times. As user numbers grow or data volume expands, a system that is not designed to scale efficiently will begin to show delays. For example, a web application that retrieves data from a database may perform flawlessly with a few dozen users but struggle as that number climbs into the thousands. Database queries that once completed in milliseconds may now take several seconds, creating a bottleneck that affects the entire application. Monitoring tools that track response times at various layers—such as the user interface, APIs, and database—can reveal where the slowdown originates. Patterns in these delays often point to areas of the system that require optimization or redesign.

Resource utilization metrics offer another critical insight into scalability. High and steadily increasing CPU, memory, or disk usage often signal that a system is nearing its capacity. A web server, for instance, might show CPU spikes during peak traffic hours, and while this may initially appear manageable, sustained high utilization can lead to degraded performance or crashes. Similarly, a database server running low on available memory might resort to slow disk-based operations, significantly increasing query execution times. These metrics also highlight inefficiencies: a service consuming excessive resources for relatively simple tasks could benefit from code optimization or architectural changes.

Concurrency limits frequently reveal themselves as systems grow. Many applications are designed to handle a fixed number of simultaneous connections or operations. A messaging platform, for example, might support 1,000 concurrent users without issue, but as that number grows to 10,000, users may start experiencing dropped connections, delayed messages, or complete service outages. These limitations can stem from constraints at various levels, such as application logic, thread pools, or external dependencies like databases and APIs. Identifying concurrency thresholds requires stress testing the system under simulated loads, uncovering the breaking points before they are encountered in production.

Error rates are another telling indicator that a system might be struggling to scale. As load increases, components that were once reliable may start to fail intermittently. Timeouts, failed database queries, or rejected requests are common symptoms. For instance, an e-commerce application experiencing a surge in traffic during a major sale might see a spike in failed transactions or incomplete user sessions. These errors are often a result of resource exhaustion, such as a thread pool reaching its maximum capacity or a database hitting its connection limit. Monitoring error rates and correlating them with system load helps pinpoint the root cause and informs decisions about where to focus scaling efforts.

Queue lengths and processing backlogs provide additional evidence of scalability challenges. Many systems rely on queues to manage tasks such as processing orders, sending notifications, or handling background jobs. When the rate at which tasks are added to the queue consistently outpaces the rate at which they are processed, it indicates a scaling problem. For example, a notification service might handle 100 requests per second during normal operation but receive 1,000 requests per second during a promotional campaign. If the service cannot process notifications as quickly as they arrive, the queue will grow indefinitely, leading to delays that impact user experience. Observing queue lengths over time helps identify components that require additional resources or more efficient processing mechanisms.

Growth in data volume is another factor that often triggers scalability concerns. As databases grow larger, operations that were previously fast can become sluggish. Searching, indexing, and retrieving data involve more overhead when dealing with millions or billions of records. An online travel platform, for instance, might face challenges as its database of flights, hotels, and user reviews expands. Without proper indexing, partitioning, or archiving strategies, the system may slow to a crawl. Tracking database growth and its impact on query performance ensures that these issues are addressed before they escalate.

User behavior patterns can also serve as early indicators of scalability needs. Changes in how users interact with the system—such as an increase in concurrent logins, longer session durations, or more frequent data uploads—can place unexpected demands on infrastructure. A photo-sharing app, for example, might see a sudden spike in uploads following the release of a new feature. Even if the infrastructure was designed to handle typical usage patterns, such shifts in behavior can expose weaknesses. Analyzing usage trends and preparing for potential surges ensures the system can adapt to evolving demands.

Dependencies on external services often reveal scalability limits as well. Many systems rely on third-party APIs, cloud services, or other external components. These dependencies may have their own constraints, such as rate limits or capacity caps. A streaming service that uses a third-party CDN to deliver video content might find itself constrained by the CDN's bandwidth allocation during a popular event. Monitoring these dependencies and understanding their limitations is crucial for building a scalable system. In some cases, redundancy or alternative providers may be necessary to ensure reliable performance under high load.

Cost metrics are a less technical but equally important indicator of scalability challenges. As a system scales, the associated costs often rise. Infrastructure, cloud services, and licensing fees can escalate rapidly if not managed carefully. For instance, an application hosted on a cloud platform might incur disproportionately high costs as traffic increases, particularly if resources are over-provisioned to handle spikes. Analyzing the relationship between cost and system performance helps identify inefficiencies and guides decisions about when and how to scale.

Scalability indicators rarely appear in isolation. High response times often coincide with increased resource utilization, growing error rates, and backlogged queues. Identifying these patterns requires comprehensive monitoring and a proactive mindset. By continuously evaluating these indicators, teams can anticipate scalability challenges and address them before they impact users. The goal is not just to react to problems but to build systems that are inherently prepared for growth, ensuring long-term success without sacrificing performance or reliability.

Security Vulnerability Recognition

Every software system, no matter how advanced, is inherently vulnerable to potential threats. Security vulnerabilities are weaknesses or flaws within a system that can be exploited to compromise its integrity, confidentiality, or availability. Recognizing these vulnerabilities is a critical first step in safeguarding applications, data, and users. The challenge lies in the fact that vulnerabilities are often subtle, hidden deep within code, configurations, or even user interactions. Identifying them requires a blend of technical expertise, careful observation, and a mindset attuned to anticipating potential exploits.

One of the most common sources of vulnerabilities lies in input handling. Systems that fail to validate, sanitize, or properly handle user input open themselves to a range of attacks, from SQL injection to cross-site scripting (XSS). For example, a login form that directly incorporates user-provided input into a database query without validation can allow an attacker to execute malicious SQL commands. While this might seem like an outdated or well-known vulnerability, it persists because even minor oversights in code can reintroduce the issue. Recognizing these weaknesses requires reviewing code with a focus on how external inputs are processed and ensuring that strict validation measures are in place.

Configuration errors are another frequent culprit. Misconfigured servers, databases, or application settings can inadvertently expose sensitive data or provide unauthorized access. Consider a cloud storage bucket that is set to "public" instead of "private." This simple misconfiguration could result in confidential files being accessible to anyone with the URL. Similarly, leaving default credentials unchanged, such as "admin/admin," provides an easy entry point for attackers. These types of vulnerabilities might not be visible in the application's code but are equally dangerous. Regular audits of configurations, combined with adherence to best practices, are essential for recognizing and addressing these oversights.

Dependencies and third-party libraries are another major area of concern. Modern software often relies on external libraries to provide functionality, from authentication frameworks to UI components. While these dependencies save time and effort, they can also introduce vulnerabilities into the system. A widely used library may contain a security flaw that, if exploited, affects every application that relies on it. For example, the Log4Shell vulnerability in the Log4j library demonstrated how a single weakness in a popular dependency could have widespread consequences. Staying vigilant requires tracking the libraries your application depends on, monitoring for known vulnerabilities, and applying updates or patches promptly.

Authentication and authorization mechanisms are critical components of any secure system, yet they are often implemented with gaps that attackers can exploit. Weak password policies, such as allowing short or commonly used passwords, make it easier for attackers to gain unauthorized access. Beyond passwords, systems that fail to enforce proper session management or token expiration leave users exposed. For instance, if an authentication token remains active indefinitely, an attacker who intercepts it can impersonate the user long after the session should have ended. Recognizing vulnerabilities in authentication involves scrutinizing how user credentials and sessions are handled, ensuring that security measures like multi-factor authentication, secure encryption, and session expiration are implemented effectively.

Brute force and denial-of-service (DoS) vulnerabilities are often overlooked until attackers exploit them. A login endpoint that allows unlimited attempts without delay is vulnerable to brute force attacks, where an attacker systematically guesses passwords until they succeed. Similarly, endpoints that fail to implement rate limiting or resource quotas may be susceptible to DoS attacks, where an attacker overwhelms the system with requests, rendering it unusable. Recognizing these vulnerabilities means thinking like an adversary, identifying areas where the system's resources or logic can be abused, and implementing countermeasures to prevent exploitation.

Error handling and logging mechanisms, while essential for debugging and monitoring, can also inadvertently expose sensitive information. Error messages that reveal stack traces, database queries, or other internal details provide attackers with valuable insights into the system's design. For example, an error message that explicitly states "Invalid username" versus "Invalid password" during a login attempt gives an attacker clues about which credentials are correct. Recognizing vulnerabilities in error handling involves reviewing what information is exposed to users and ensuring that logs containing sensitive data are securely stored and accessible only to authorized personnel.

The human factor is often the weakest link in security. Social engineering attacks, such as phishing or pretexting, exploit human psychology rather than technical flaws. Even the most secure system can be compromised if an attacker convinces an employee to share their login credentials or click on a malicious link. Recognizing vulnerabilities related to the human factor involves analyzing workflows, identifying areas where users might be manipulated, and implementing training programs to raise awareness about security risks.

Network-level vulnerabilities present another layer of risk, especially for applications that communicate over the internet. Unencrypted data transmitted between a client and server can be intercepted and manipulated by attackers using techniques like man-in-the-middle (MITM) attacks. For instance, a user accessing a website over an unsecured HTTP connection may unknowingly expose their login credentials. Recognizing these vulnerabilities requires a thorough understanding of how data is transmitted and ensuring the use of secure protocols such as HTTPS, along with additional measures like SSL/TLS certificates.

Legacy systems and outdated software are particularly prone to vulnerabilities. Older systems often lack modern security features and may no longer receive updates or patches. An outdated content management system, for example, might contain known vulnerabilities that attackers can easily exploit. Recognizing vulnerabilities in legacy systems involves assessing their current state, identifying any unpatched issues, and determining whether they should be updated, replaced, or isolated from critical infrastructure.

The process of recognizing security vulnerabilities is not static. Threat landscapes evolve, and new attack vectors emerge as technology advances. What was considered secure yesterday might be vulnerable today. This dynamic nature of threats underscores the importance of ongoing vigilance. Regular penetration testing, code reviews, and threat modeling sessions help uncover vulnerabilities that might otherwise go unnoticed. For example, simulating an attack on a system can reveal overlooked weaknesses, allowing them to be addressed before a real attacker discovers them.

Recognizing security vulnerabilities is not merely a technical skill but a mindset. It requires the ability to anticipate how systems can be misused and the discipline to continually evaluate and improve defenses. Every vulnerability identified and addressed strengthens the system, protecting users, data, and the organization as a whole. By approaching security as an ongoing process rather than a one-time task, organizations can stay ahead of potential threats and build systems that are both resilient and trustworthy.

Integration Point Analysis

The success of any modern software system often hinges on how well its individual components work together. Integration points—where these components interact with one another or with external systems—serve as the connective tissue of a system's architecture. These points are critical because they facilitate the flow of data, commands, and responses, ensuring the system operates cohesively. However, they are simultaneously areas of vulnerability. Poorly designed or inadequately analyzed integration points can result in failures, performance bottlenecks, or security breaches. Understanding and analyzing these points is therefore a vital step in creating a robust and reliable system.

Integration points come in many forms, from API calls and database connections to third-party services and message queues. Each of these represents a boundary between two or more systems, and the way these boundaries are managed has significant implications for functionality and performance. Consider, for example, a payment gateway integrated into an e-commerce platform. This gateway represents an external integration point, where the platform must send and receive data securely and reliably. If the integration is not thoroughly analyzed, issues such as transaction failures, latency, or data inconsistencies can arise, directly impacting the user experience and the business's revenue. The same principles apply to internal integration points, such as a microservice architecture where individual services exchange data with one another. Any inefficiency or fault in these exchanges can ripple throughout the entire system.

One of the first steps in analyzing integration points is identifying the data flows and dependencies involved. Every integration point relies on specific inputs and outputs, and understanding these is essential for evaluating potential risks. For instance, a customer relationship management (CRM) system that pulls data from a central database depends on the availability and consistency of that data. If the database experiences delays or corruption, the CRM system's functionality will be compromised. Mapping out these data flows reveals not only the direct dependencies but also the cascading effects that can occur when one component fails. This kind of analysis highlights critical points that require additional safeguards, such as redundancy or failover mechanisms.

Performance is another key factor to consider when analyzing integration points. The speed and efficiency with which components interact determine the overall responsiveness of the system. Imagine a logistics platform where a warehouse management system (WMS) communicates with an inventory tracking system to update stock levels. If the integration point between these two systems involves slow or poorly optimized queries, the delay will propagate through the entire workflow, potentially causing shipment delays and customer dissatisfaction. Performance testing at integration points helps uncover such bottlenecks, allowing developers to optimize queries, streamline communication protocols, or even redesign the integration architecture if necessary.

Error handling is a critical aspect of integration point analysis. No system is immune to failures, and integration points are often where they become most apparent. A weather application, for example, might rely on an external API to fetch real-time weather data. If the API becomes unavailable or returns unexpected results, the application must have mechanisms in place to handle these errors gracefully. Without proper error handling, a failure at the integration point could cause the entire application to crash or display incorrect data. Robust analysis involves considering all possible failure scenarios—timeouts, incorrect data formats, or partial responses—and designing fallback strategies to minimize their impact. These strategies could include retries, default values, or even user notifications to ensure transparency.

Security is another crucial dimension of integration point analysis. Every interaction between systems represents a potential attack surface, and integration points are particularly attractive targets for malicious actors. Take, for instance, an online banking platform that integrates with a third-party authentication service. If the communication between these systems is not encrypted or properly authenticated, it could be intercepted and exploited by attackers. Security analysis should focus on ensuring that data transmitted across integration points is encrypted, access is restricted to authorized entities, and vulnerabilities such as injection attacks are mitigated. Regular audits and penetration testing of integration points can further strengthen their resilience.

Scalability is often overlooked during initial integration point design but becomes a pressing issue as systems grow. A content delivery platform, for instance, might initially integrate with a single image processing service to handle uploads. As user numbers increase, the integration point may struggle to keep up with the volume of requests, leading to delays or failures. Analyzing integration points for scalability involves evaluating whether they can handle increased loads and identifying potential bottlenecks. Solutions might include load balancing, caching, or sharding to distribute workloads more effectively. By addressing scalability early on, systems can avoid costly reengineering efforts down the line.

Another important consideration is the compatibility and versioning of systems interacting at integration points. Over time, external APIs, libraries, or services may update or deprecate features, potentially breaking existing integrations. For example, a social media platform might update its API, changing how user data is retrieved. If the dependent system does not adapt to these changes, the integration point will fail. Proactive analysis involves monitoring for updates or deprecations and designing systems with backward compatibility or adaptability in mind. This ensures that integrations remain functional even as underlying systems evolve.

Monitoring and observability also play a vital role in integration point analysis. Without visibility into how these points are performing, it's impossible to detect or resolve issues effectively. A distributed e-commerce platform, for instance, might have multiple integration points involving inventory systems, payment gateways, and shipping services. Monitoring tools that track metrics such as latency, error rates, and throughput provide real-time insights into the health of these integration points. When anomalies occur—such as a sudden spike in response times or an increase in failed requests—these tools enable rapid diagnosis and resolution. Observability enhances the ability to maintain system reliability, even as complexities grow.

Integration points also have a qualitative dimension: they shape how teams collaborate and manage dependencies. In systems involving multiple teams or organizations, such as a supply chain network, integration points must be clearly defined and documented. Ambiguity in data formats, protocols, or error codes can lead to miscommunication and inefficiency. Establishing clear contracts or service-level agreements (SLAs) for integration points fosters alignment and accountability among all parties involved. For example, specifying that an API will respond within 200 milliseconds or provide detailed error messages ensures that expectations are met and misunderstandings are minimized.

Analyzing integration points is not a one-time task but an ongoing process. As systems evolve, new integration points are added, and existing ones face changing demands. Continuous evaluation ensures that these critical connections remain reliable, secure, and efficient. By dedicating attention to integration point analysis, developers and architects can build systems that are not only technically sound but also resilient to the challenges of growth, complexity, and change. This approach lays the groundwork for systems that are seamless, scalable, and capable of enduring the demands of an interconnected digital ecosystem.

Chapter 6: The Human Element in Code

Reading Developer Intent

Understanding developer intent is an essential skill for anyone working within a collaborative or inherited codebase. Every line of code, every function, and every architectural decision reflects choices made by a developer to solve a specific problem or fulfill a particular requirement. However, these intentions are not always immediately obvious, especially in complex systems or poorly documented projects. Misinterpreting them can lead to inefficient debugging, flawed modifications, or even the introduction of new errors. To navigate this challenge, it's crucial to develop the ability to discern what the original developer was trying to achieve, why they made certain choices, and how those decisions fit into the broader goals of the system.

The first step in reading developer intent is to approach the code with the right mindset. Rather than assuming the code is flawed or unnecessarily complicated, it's helpful to begin with the assumption that the developer had a valid reason for writing it the way they did. This shift in perspective encourages curiosity and reduces the frustration that often accompanies working with unfamiliar code. For example, encountering a seemingly convoluted algorithm might initially feel like overengineering. However, upon deeper inspection, you might discover that it was designed to handle edge cases you hadn't considered, such as specific performance constraints or compatibility issues. Recognizing that every snippet of code is there to solve a problem—even if it's not immediately clear what that problem is—sets the stage for uncovering the underlying intent.

Context plays a significant role in deciphering developer intent. Code does not exist in isolation; it is always part of a larger system, influenced by requirements, constraints, and timelines. To understand why a developer wrote something in a particular way, it's essential to consider the broader circumstances surrounding its creation. Was the system designed during a time when certain technologies were dominant? Were there limitations in hardware or software that dictated specific approaches? For instance, older systems may include cryptic optimizations aimed at conserving memory because they were developed in an era when memory was expensive and scarce. Without this historical context, modern developers might dismiss these optimizations as unnecessary complexity. Understanding the environment in which the code was written can shed light on decisions that might otherwise seem perplexing.

Documentation, when available, serves as a valuable window into developer intent. Comments within the code, design documents, or even commit messages often provide insights into the reasoning behind specific implementations. However, these artifacts are not always complete or accurate, and sometimes they can be misleading. A comment might describe what the code is supposed to do, but not why it was written that way. Conversely, commit messages might explain the motivation for a change but omit technical details.

Combining multiple sources of documentation and cross-referencing them with the actual code is often necessary to piece together a coherent understanding. For example, if a comment mentions a "temporary fix for bug #1234," reviewing the bug tracker can provide additional context about the issue and why the fix was implemented in that manner.

Patterns and conventions within the codebase offer another layer of insight. Developers often rely on consistent naming schemes, architectural patterns, or stylistic choices that reflect their thought processes. Recognizing these patterns can help you infer intent even when explicit documentation is lacking. For instance, a codebase might use a specific naming convention where variables prefixed with "temp" indicate temporary storage. Understanding this convention allows you to immediately identify the purpose of such variables without needing to trace their entire lifecycle. Similarly, adherence to design patterns, such as Model-View-Controller (MVC) or Dependency Injection, can provide clues about the intended separation of concerns or the flow of data through the system.

Edge cases and error handling routines often reveal the depth of a developer's intent. These sections of code demonstrate an awareness of potential issues and a proactive approach to addressing them. For example, a function that validates user input might include checks for scenarios such as null values, invalid formats, or malicious payloads. By examining these checks, you can infer that the developer anticipated specific risks and took steps to mitigate them. On the other hand, the absence of robust error handling might suggest that the developer was working under tight deadlines or assumed that the input would always be well-formed. In either case, these details provide a glimpse into the priorities and assumptions that shaped the code.

Understanding trade-offs is another key aspect of reading developer intent. Every decision in software development involves compromises, whether between performance and readability, flexibility and simplicity, or short-term needs and long-term maintainability. For example, a developer might choose to hard-code certain values instead of making them configurable because the system was initially intended for limited use. Over time, as requirements evolve, these hard-coded values may become problematic, but their presence reflects a decision that was likely justified at the time. Recognizing these trade-offs helps you appreciate the rationale behind the code and informs your own decisions when modifying or extending it.

Collaboration and communication can also provide valuable insights into developer intent. When working directly with the original developer, asking targeted questions can clarify ambiguities and uncover the reasoning behind specific choices. Even when the original developer is no longer available, team members who worked on adjacent components or reviewed the code might offer useful context. For instance, a team discussion about performance bottlenecks might explain why certain optimizations were prioritized over others. These interpersonal exchanges often reveal nuances that are not captured in the code or documentation.

Reading developer intent requires not just technical skills but also empathy and a willingness to learn from the perspectives of others. Every piece of code represents hours of thought, problem-solving, and decision-making. By approaching it with an open mind and a methodical process, you can uncover the logic and purpose behind even the most bewildering implementations. This understanding not only allows you to work more effectively within the codebase but also fosters a sense of respect for the challenges and constraints faced by those who came before you. Interpreting intent is not merely an exercise in deciphering code; it is a means of connecting with the creative process of software development and contributing to its ongoing evolution.

Code Style as Communication

Code style is more than a matter of aesthetics or personal preference; it serves as a universal language within a team, a way for developers to communicate ideas, intentions, and expectations to one another. While machines will execute code regardless of its formatting or structure, humans depend on clarity and consistency to understand and maintain it. A well-defined code style enhances readability, reduces misunderstandings, and fosters collaboration, making it one of the most critical aspects of software development. When developers adhere to a shared style, they create an environment where code becomes approachable, even for those who didn't write it.

Consider a scenario where a team inherits a legacy codebase written without consistent conventions.

Variable names vary wildly in format—some are camelCase, others snake_case, and a few are inexplicably abbreviated to a point of incomprehension. Nested loops and conditional statements lack consistent indentation, creating a maze of logic that requires painstaking effort to unravel. Even the most skilled developer would struggle to decipher such a codebase without first expending significant time and energy untangling its structure. These frustrations highlight how poor code style can act as a barrier to understanding, slowing progress and increasing the likelihood of errors.

Clarity is at the heart of code style as communication. Each line of code should convey its purpose in a way that is immediately understandable to its intended audience. Naming conventions play a pivotal role here. A variable named userData provides far more insight than one named x. Similarly, a function named calculateTax is inherently more descriptive than one named doStuff. Choosing clear, meaningful names requires developers to think critically about the role each variable, function, or class plays within the system. This clarity reduces cognitive load, enabling team members to focus on solving problems rather than deciphering cryptic code.

Consistency amplifies the **benefits** of clarity. A single developer might write clear and readable code in isolation, but if their style differs significantly from that of their teammates, the codebase can quickly become fragmented and disjointed. Imagine working in a system where one module uses tabs for indentation, while another uses spaces. Or where some functions place opening braces on a new line, while others keep them on the same line. These inconsistencies force developers to constantly switch mental gears as they navigate the code, leading to frustration and errors. A consistent style acts as a unifying thread, ensuring that the codebase feels cohesive and predictable, no matter who contributed to it.

Code style also communicates intent. The way a developer structures their code can reveal their priorities, assumptions, and understanding of the problem they are solving. For example, a function with a detailed comment explaining its purpose and edge cases signals that the developer anticipated potential confusion and took steps to address it. Conversely, a function with no comments and a name like processData might leave future maintainers guessing what it actually does. The use of whitespace, too, can suggest how the developer intended the code to be read. A well-placed line break between logical blocks of code creates a natural pause, guiding the reader's attention and emphasizing the separation of concerns.

Beyond readability, code style plays a critical role in fostering collaboration. In team environments, developers often work on the same codebase simultaneously, submitting changes, reviewing each other's work, and merging updates. A shared code style ensures that these interactions occur smoothly, minimizing friction and misunderstandings. When a pull request adheres to established conventions, the reviewer can focus on the substance of the changes rather than being distracted by formatting issues. This alignment creates a sense of trust and professionalism within the team, reinforcing the idea that everyone is working toward the same goals.

Establishing and maintaining a consistent code style requires deliberate effort. Teams often adopt style guides tailored to their programming language or framework, defining conventions for everything from indentation and spacing to naming and file organization. These guides serve as a reference point, ensuring that everyone is aligned on best practices. However, the true value of a style guide lies not in its strict enforcement but in the shared understanding it creates. Developers who participate in discussions about style decisions are more likely to feel invested in adhering to them, knowing that the guidelines reflect their collective input and expertise.

Tools can also play a vital role in reinforcing code style. Linters, formatters, and integrated development environments (IDEs) can automatically enforce conventions, catching deviations before they become a problem. These tools remove the burden of policing style from individual developers, freeing them to focus on higher-level concerns. For instance, a linter might flag a variable name that doesn't conform to the agreed-upon convention, prompting the developer to correct it before committing their changes. By automating these checks, teams can maintain a high standard of style without resorting to tedious and subjective code reviews.

While adhering to a consistent style is essential, it's equally important to recognize when flexibility is needed. Codebases evolve over time, and so do the teams that maintain them. A style that made sense when the project was small might no longer be practical as it scales. For example, a rule requiring detailed comments on every function might slow development unnecessarily once the team grows familiar with the codebase. Periodically revisiting and updating style guidelines ensures that they remain relevant and effective, balancing the needs of clarity, consistency, and efficiency.

Code style as communication extends beyond the immediate team. Open-source projects, for instance, rely heavily on clear and consistent style to attract contributors and encourage collaboration. A well-structured codebase with a clear style guide invites involvement, signaling that the maintainers care about quality and are committed to making the project accessible. Conversely, a disorganized or inconsistent codebase can deter potential contributors, who may perceive it as unmanageable or poorly maintained. In this way, code style serves as a bridge between developers, fostering a sense of community and shared purpose.

Documentation Psychology

Documentation often carries a misunderstood reputation among developers. While some treat it as an afterthought, others view it as a burdensome chore that takes time away from coding. Yet, documentation is not merely a technical artifact; it is a reflection of how developers think, communicate, and empathize with others who will interact with their work. The psychology behind documentation reveals the interplay between cognitive processes, team dynamics, and the long-term sustainability of a project. Understanding this psychology is essential to creating documentation that not only informs but also connects with its audience effectively.

At its core, documentation serves as a bridge between the people who create a system and those who use, maintain, or extend it. This bridge must account for the knowledge gap that inevitably exists between these groups. The creator of a system is intimately familiar with its intricacies, often to the point where certain details feel too obvious to document. However, what seems apparent to the creator may be entirely opaque to someone approaching the system for the first time. This phenomenon, sometimes referred to as the curse of knowledge, illustrates why documentation must be written with empathy. The writer must step outside their own expertise and consider the perspective of a reader who knows nothing about the system. This requires not only technical skill but also an ability to anticipate questions, frustrations, and misunderstandings.

The structure and tone of documentation often reflect the mindset of the person who wrote it. Concise, well-organized documentation suggests a developer who values clarity and understands the importance of guiding others through complex systems. Conversely, disjointed or overly verbose documentation may indicate either a rushed effort or an underlying uncertainty about the system itself. In this way, documentation acts as a mirror, revealing not just the technical aspects of a project but also the thought processes and priorities of its creators. This is why documentation is often considered a sign of a team's maturity. A team that invests in clear and comprehensive documentation demonstrates a commitment to collaboration, knowledge sharing, and long-term success.

The psychological burden of poor documentation is significant. Imagine inheriting a codebase with minimal or outdated documentation. The initial experience is likely one of frustration and confusion, as you struggle to piece together the system's functionality and purpose. This cognitive load not only slows progress but also creates a sense of isolation, as you lack the guidance that good documentation provides. Over time, this frustration can lead to a negative association with the project itself, reducing motivation and increasing the likelihood of errors. Well-crafted documentation, on the other hand, reduces this cognitive load by offering a clear roadmap. It provides context, explains relationships, and answers questions before they arise, creating an environment where the developer feels supported rather than overwhelmed.

The act of writing documentation is itself a cognitive process that benefits the author as much as the reader. Translating complex ideas into clear, written explanations forces the writer to organize their thoughts and identify gaps in their understanding. Many developers have experienced the phenomenon where attempting to document a feature reveals edge cases or inconsistencies that were previously overlooked. This is because writing documentation requires a shift from implicit to explicit knowledge. Implicit knowledge resides in the mind of the developer, often in a fragmented and intuitive form.

Explicit knowledge, by contrast, is structured and accessible, making it easier to share and refine. In this way, documentation not only communicates information to others but also deepens the author's own understanding of the system.

The psychological impact of documentation extends to team dynamics. In collaborative environments, documentation serves as a shared resource that reduces dependency on individual team members. Without it, teams often rely on tribal knowledge— information that is known by a few but not documented for the group. This creates bottlenecks, as those with the knowledge become gatekeepers, and others must constantly seek their input. Over time, this dynamic can lead to burnout for the gatekeepers and frustration for those who feel excluded from the flow of information. Comprehensive documentation democratizes knowledge, ensuring that everyone has equal access to the information they need to contribute effectively. It fosters a sense of autonomy and empowerment, as team members can resolve their own questions without relying on others.

The tone of documentation also plays a crucial role in its effectiveness. Documentation that is overly technical or condescending can alienate readers, making them feel inadequate or unwelcome. A more approachable tone, by contrast, creates a sense of collaboration and mutual respect. For example, a troubleshooting guide that acknowledges common mistakes without judgment encourages readers to experiment and learn without fear of failure. This psychological safety is especially important for newcomers, who may already feel intimidated by the complexity of the system. By framing documentation as a conversation rather than a lecture, writers can create a more inclusive and supportive experience.

The relationship between documentation and trust cannot be overstated. When documentation is clear, accurate, and up-to-date, it signals to users and maintainers that the system itself is reliable and well-maintained. Conversely, incomplete or outdated documentation raises red flags, suggesting that the system may be neglected or poorly understood. This erosion of trust can have far-reaching consequences, from reluctance to adopt the system to skepticism about its long-term viability. Maintaining documentation is therefore not just a technical task but a way of building and preserving trust within the development community.

Tools and processes can support the psychological aspects of documentation, but they cannot replace the human effort required to make it effective. Automated tools can generate API references or extract comments from code, but these outputs often lack the context and nuance that only a human writer can provide. Good documentation anticipates the needs of its audience, weaving together technical details, examples, and explanations in a way that feels coherent and purposeful. Achieving this level of quality requires time, attention, and a genuine desire to help others succeed.

Chapter 7: Future Proofing and Innovation

Emerging Pattern Detection

Patterns are the backbone of understanding and decision-making in software development. Detecting them early and accurately can mean the difference between a system that evolves gracefully and one that collapses under its own weight. Emerging pattern detection refers to the ability to identify trends, recurring structures, or behaviors within a codebase, system, or process before they become entrenched. These patterns often provide valuable insights into how a system is being used, how it is likely to grow, and where potential risks or opportunities may lie. Understanding and acting on these patterns is essential for maintaining sustainable, efficient, and scalable systems.

Patterns rarely announce themselves with fanfare. Instead, they emerge quietly over time, often disguised as isolated events or anomalies. A developer might notice that certain types of bugs keep appearing in the same module, or that new features consistently require changes to a specific set of files. At first glance, these occurrences may seem unrelated or coincidental. But when viewed through the lens of pattern detection, they begin to reveal deeper truths about the system's architecture and the behaviors of the people interacting with it. Recognizing these early hints requires a combination of keen observation, analytical thinking, and a willingness to question assumptions.

One of the most common areas where emerging patterns become apparent is in the way code evolves over time. For instance, a particular function may start as a simple utility but gradually accumulate additional responsibilities as developers add features or handle edge cases. What began as a clean, single-purpose function transforms into a sprawling, multifaceted one, commonly referred to as a "god function." Detecting this pattern early allows teams to refactor the code before it becomes unmanageable, splitting it into smaller, more focused components. This not only improves maintainability but also prevents the pattern from proliferating across the codebase.

Another area where patterns often emerge is in dependencies. Modern software systems rely heavily on external libraries, frameworks, and services. Over time, certain dependencies may start to dominate the system, either because they are used in multiple places or because they become deeply integrated into critical workflows. For example, a web application might increasingly lean on a third-party authentication service. While this dependency might make sense initially, its growing influence could create risks, such as vendor lock-in or reduced flexibility. Detecting this pattern early allows teams to evaluate whether the dependency aligns with the system's long-term goals and, if necessary, explore alternatives.

Patterns also emerge in the way teams work together. Communication habits, workflows, and decision-making processes often leave traces in the code. For example, if a particular team consistently works on a specific module, that module may start to reflect the team's unique preferences or biases. This can lead to siloed knowledge, where only certain team members understand how the module functions. Detecting this pattern early provides an opportunity to address it through documentation, cross-training, or even restructuring team responsibilities. By doing so, teams can avoid bottlenecks and ensure that knowledge is distributed more evenly.

Testing practices are another fertile ground for pattern detection. Over time, certain types of tests may receive more attention than others, creating an imbalance in the test suite. For instance, a team might focus heavily on unit tests while neglecting integration or performance tests. This imbalance often reflects an underlying pattern in the team's priorities, constraints, or assumptions. Detecting this trend allows the team to course-correct, ensuring that the test suite provides comprehensive coverage and aligns with the system's needs.

Monitoring and observability tools provide a wealth of data for detecting emerging patterns in system behavior. Metrics such as response times, error rates, and resource utilization often reveal trends that are not immediately obvious. For example, a gradual increase in database query times might indicate that a particular table is becoming a bottleneck as the system scales. Similarly, a spike in error rates during specific hours might point to usage patterns that were not anticipated during development. Detecting these patterns early allows teams to address issues proactively, whether by optimizing queries, scaling infrastructure, or adjusting workflows.

Security is another domain where pattern detection is invaluable. Attackers often rely on predictable behaviors or overlooked vulnerabilities to exploit systems. For instance, a sudden increase in login attempts from a specific IP range might indicate the beginning of a brute-force attack. Similarly, repeated access to certain endpoints could suggest that an attacker is probing the system for weaknesses. Detecting these patterns early enables teams to respond quickly, implementing measures such as rate limiting or enhanced authentication protocols to mitigate the threat.

Emerging patterns are not always negative; they can also highlight opportunities for improvement or innovation. For example, if user feedback consistently mentions a specific pain point, this trend might indicate an area where the system could be improved. Similarly, if a particular feature is being used in ways that were not originally intended, this pattern might suggest an opportunity to expand or refine the feature. Detecting these positive patterns requires paying close attention to feedback, usage data, and other signals that reveal how the system is being received and adapted by its users.

Detecting emerging patterns is as much an art as it is a science. While tools and metrics can provide valuable data, the ability to interpret that data and identify meaningful trends often depends on intuition and experience. Developers who hone this skill gain a powerful advantage, as they can anticipate issues and opportunities before they become obvious. This proactive approach not only improves the quality of the system but also reduces stress and uncertainty, as teams are better prepared to navigate the complexities of software development.

The process of detecting patterns is iterative and ongoing. Systems evolve, teams change, and new challenges emerge, requiring constant vigilance and adaptability. By cultivating an awareness of emerging patterns, developers and teams can stay ahead of the curve, addressing issues before they escalate and capitalizing on opportunities as they arise. This mindset transforms software development from a reactive process into a proactive one, where patterns are not just identified but understood and leveraged to create systems that are both resilient and innovative.

Extensibility Assessment

Extensibility is one of the defining characteristics of robust software systems. It determines whether a system can adapt to changing requirements, accommodate new features, and integrate with emerging technologies without a complete overhaul. Assessing extensibility is not merely about evaluating how a system might grow but understanding how its current design choices enable or hinder that growth. It requires a deep dive into architectural decisions, code structure, and the underlying principles that guide the system's evolution. The ability to assess extensibility effectively can save a project from stagnation, ensuring it remains relevant and functional in an ever-changing landscape.

Every extensible system begins with a foundation of modularity. Modules, whether they are components, classes, or services, encapsulate specific functionality and provide clear interfaces for interaction. By design, these modules reduce dependencies and create boundaries that make it easier to modify or extend individual parts of the system without affecting others. An extensibility assessment often starts by examining the degree of modularity within the system. A codebase where functionality is tightly coupled, with one module directly relying on the internal details of another, signals a lack of foresight. Such coupling creates a domino effect: changing one part of the system necessitates changes in others, leading to brittle and inflexible designs. In contrast, a well-modularized system allows developers to introduce new features by creating or extending modules without disrupting the existing structure.

The clarity and consistency of interfaces play a pivotal role in extensibility. Interfaces, whether they are APIs, communication protocols, or method signatures, define how different parts of a system interact. To assess extensibility, one must evaluate whether these interfaces are designed with future growth in mind. A rigid interface that tightly binds its users to a specific implementation limits the system's ability to evolve. For example, an API that hardcodes response formats or omits versioning mechanisms can become a roadblock as new requirements emerge. On the other hand, interfaces that are abstract, well-documented, and forward-compatible create the flexibility needed to adapt without breaking existing functionality. They serve as contracts that allow different parts of the system to evolve independently while maintaining compatibility.

Another essential aspect of extensibility assessment is the examination of abstraction layers within the system. Abstraction provides a means to separate high-level functionality from low-level implementation details, creating a buffer that shields the system from changes in underlying technologies. For instance, a database abstraction layer allows developers to replace a relational database with a NoSQL solution without rewriting the entire application. However, abstraction should be applied judiciously. Over-abstraction can lead to unnecessary complexity and performance overhead, while under-abstraction makes the system rigid and harder to extend. A balanced approach, where abstractions are introduced to manage complexity without obscuring functionality, is the hallmark of an extensible system.

Dependency management is another critical factor in assessing extensibility. Dependencies, whether internal or external, are both a strength and a risk. While they enable reuse and accelerate development, they can also introduce constraints that limit how a system can grow. An extensibility assessment involves identifying these dependencies and evaluating their impact on future changes. For example, a system heavily reliant on a specific third-party library might face challenges if that library becomes deprecated or incompatible with new requirements. Dependency injection, loose coupling, and clear documentation of dependencies are strategies that mitigate these risks, creating a system that can adapt even as its ecosystem evolves.

Flexibility in configuration and customization is a direct indicator of a system's readiness to accommodate change. Systems that rely on hard-coded values or rigid workflows often struggle to adapt, as even minor changes require modifying the codebase. In contrast, a system that provides configuration files, environment variables, or plugin architectures empowers users to adapt it to new contexts without altering its core. For example, a web application that allows developers to add custom middleware or define routing rules in configuration files can accommodate diverse use cases without requiring a rewrite. An extensibility assessment should examine how easily the system can be tailored to meet new requirements and whether these mechanisms are intuitive and well-documented.

Backward compatibility is another dimension of extensibility that cannot be overlooked. Adding new features or adapting to new standards is only valuable if it doesn't disrupt existing functionality. An extensibility assessment evaluates whether the system includes mechanisms for maintaining compatibility, such as feature flags, versioned APIs, or migration tools. These mechanisms ensure that current users can continue using the system while new capabilities are introduced incrementally. Backward compatibility reflects a mature approach to extensibility, where growth is managed in a way that respects the needs of both current and future users.

Scalability and performance considerations are intertwined with extensibility. A system that cannot handle increased loads or larger datasets will struggle to grow, no matter how modular or flexible its design may be. An extensibility assessment must consider whether the system's architecture can scale horizontally, vertically, or both. For example, a system designed with distributed processing in mind can handle growth more effectively than one that relies on a single monolithic process. Similarly, performance bottlenecks, such as inefficient algorithms or poorly optimized queries, can limit a system's capacity to extend its functionality. Addressing scalability and performance issues early ensures that extensibility is not constrained by technical limitations.

Finally, the cultural and process-oriented aspects of extensibility cannot be ignored. A system's ability to grow often depends as much on the practices of the team maintaining it as on its technical design. An extensibility assessment should consider whether the team follows practices such as code reviews, continuous integration, and comprehensive testing. These practices create an environment where changes can be introduced safely and iteratively, reducing the risks associated with extending the system. Additionally, the presence of clear documentation, both for the codebase and for the processes surrounding its development, ensures that new contributors can quickly understand and build upon the existing work.

Extensibility is not a static quality but a dynamic one. It requires ongoing attention and adaptation as the system evolves. By thoroughly assessing modularity, interfaces, abstraction, dependency management, configuration, backward compatibility, scalability, and team practices, developers can identify both strengths and weaknesses in a system's design. This proactive approach ensures that the system remains capable of adapting to new challenges and opportunities, preserving its relevance and value over time. An extensible system is not just a technical achievement; it is a testament to thoughtful design and a forward-thinking mindset that prioritizes growth, adaptability, and resilience.

Technology Evolution Awareness

Technology evolves at a rate that often outpaces the ability of individuals, teams, and even organizations to fully adapt. Remaining aware of this evolution is not a luxury but a necessity, particularly in fields where innovation drives competition and success. Awareness of how technologies shift, mature, and disrupt can inform better decision-making, enable strategic planning, and ensure that systems and skills remain relevant over time. This awareness is not just about keeping up with the latest trends; it is about understanding the broader shifts in the technological landscape and their implications.

Every technology has a lifecycle. It begins with innovation, where a novel idea or breakthrough emerges, often in response to a specific problem or limitation in existing solutions. During this phase, the technology is typically unrefined, experimental, and adopted only by early adopters willing to take on the associated risks. Awareness of this phase requires curiosity and a willingness to explore uncharted territory. However, it also demands caution, as not every innovation matures into a viable or sustainable solution. For example, many frameworks and tools emerge with great promise, only to fade into obscurity when they fail to gain traction or address their intended challenges effectively.

As a technology matures, it transitions into broader adoption. This phase is characterized by increased stability, improved usability, and growing community support. Awareness during this stage involves recognizing when a technology has moved beyond its experimental roots and is becoming a standard within its domain. For instance, when cloud computing first emerged, it was met with skepticism and hesitancy. Over time, as providers enhanced security, scalability, and integration, it became a cornerstone of modern infrastructure. Being attuned to such transitions allows teams to adopt technologies at the right moment—neither too early, when risks dominate, nor too late, when competitors have already gained an advantage.

Technology evolution is not linear. Disruptions occur when new paradigms challenge existing norms, rendering established methods obsolete. These disruptions often come from unexpected directions, driven by advancements in adjacent fields or the convergence of previously unrelated ideas. For example, the rise of containerization disrupted traditional virtualization approaches, offering a lightweight and flexible alternative that revolutionized application deployment. Awareness of such disruptions requires vigilance and a willingness to question long-held assumptions. It involves looking beyond immediate needs and considering how emerging technologies might reshape the landscape in both predictable and unforeseen ways.

Staying aware of technology evolution is not solely about external observation. Internal factors, such as the systems and processes already in place, play a significant role in determining how effectively an organization can adapt. Legacy systems, while often reliable and deeply integrated, can become barriers to adopting new technologies. Awareness involves assessing whether these systems are helping or hindering progress. For example, a company relying on outdated on-premises servers might struggle to adopt modern cloud-based solutions, not because the technology isn't viable, but because of the inertia created by legacy investments. Recognizing these internal limitations allows organizations to plan transitions more effectively, ensuring that they remain agile in the face of change.

Community and ecosystem dynamics are another critical element of technology evolution awareness. The success and longevity of a technology often depend on the strength of its surrounding ecosystem—the developers, contributors, and companies that support and extend it. Observing the growth or decline of these communities can provide early indications of a technology's trajectory. For example, an open-source project with an active and engaged community is more likely to thrive than one with sporadic contributions and limited adoption. Awareness of these dynamics helps teams identify which technologies are worth investing in and which may be approaching their end of life.

Economic and industry trends also shape technology evolution. Cost, accessibility, and market demand influence which technologies gain widespread adoption and which remain niche. Awareness involves not only tracking these trends but also understanding their implications. For instance, the decreasing cost of storage and processing power has enabled the rise of big data and machine learning, fields that were previously constrained by hardware limitations. Similarly, shifts in regulatory environments, such as data privacy laws, can drive the adoption of technologies that prioritize compliance and security. Awareness of these broader forces ensures that decisions are informed by both technical and business considerations.

While staying informed about technology evolution is essential, it can also be overwhelming. The sheer volume of new tools, frameworks, and methodologies introduced each year makes it impossible to track everything. Effective awareness requires discernment—the ability to filter noise and focus on what is most relevant to your domain, team, or project. This often involves setting priorities based on strategic goals. For example, a team focused on building scalable web applications might prioritize advancements in serverless architectures over developments in low-level hardware programming. By aligning awareness efforts with specific objectives, teams can avoid the pitfalls of chasing every trend and instead concentrate on what truly matters.

Collaboration and knowledge sharing are powerful tools for maintaining awareness. Engaging with peers, attending conferences, participating in online communities, and seeking out diverse perspectives can provide valuable insights into how technologies are evolving. These interactions often reveal patterns and trends that might not be immediately apparent from individual observation. For example, a developer attending a conference might learn about an emerging framework that addresses a common pain point, sparking ideas for how it could be applied in their own work. Such exchanges enrich awareness by exposing individuals and teams to a broader range of experiences and viewpoints.

Adaptability is the natural outcome of sustained awareness. When teams and organizations remain attuned to how technologies evolve, they are better equipped to pivot when necessary. This adaptability is not about being reactive but about creating a culture of readiness. It involves cultivating skills, processes, and mindsets that embrace change as an opportunity rather than a threat. For example, a team that recognizes the growing importance of automation might invest in learning DevOps practices long before they become an industry standard, positioning themselves as leaders rather than followers.

Adaptation Strategies

Adaptation in software development is not simply about reacting to change; it is about embracing it as an inevitable and integral part of the process. Change comes in many forms—shifting requirements, emerging technologies, evolving user expectations, or unforeseen challenges—and the ability to adapt determines the longevity and success of a system or team. Strategies for adaptation involve more than technical solutions; they encompass mindset, processes, and practices that allow developers and organizations to navigate uncertainty with confidence and agility.

The first step in building effective adaptation strategies is cultivating a mindset that views change not as a disruption but as an opportunity. Resistance to change often stems from fear—fear of the unknown, fear of failure, or fear of losing control. However, teams that approach change with curiosity and openness are better positioned to discover its potential benefits. For example, a sudden shift in user requirements might initially seem like an obstacle, but it can also provide valuable insights into user needs and priorities that were not previously understood. By reframing change as a chance to learn and improve, teams can shift from a defensive posture to a proactive one.

Flexibility in architecture and design is one of the most critical technical strategies for adaptation. A rigid, tightly coupled system leaves little room for growth or modification, while a system built with extensibility in mind can accommodate changes with minimal disruption. Designing for adaptability means anticipating that requirements will evolve and creating structures that allow for incremental updates rather than wholesale rewrites. For instance, employing design patterns such as dependency injection, modular architecture, or event-driven systems can make it easier to introduce new features or replace components without affecting the entire system. These approaches ensure that the system can grow organically, responding to changing demands while maintaining stability.

Feedback loops are another cornerstone of effective adaptation. Without timely and accurate feedback, teams cannot assess whether their actions align with desired outcomes or identify areas for improvement. Feedback can come from a variety of sources: user behavior, system performance metrics, code reviews, testing, and even team retrospectives. For example, automated monitoring tools that track application performance can reveal bottlenecks or inefficiencies that need to be addressed. Similarly, user feedback collected through surveys or analytics can highlight features that require refinement or enhancements. Establishing continuous feedback loops ensures that teams remain informed and can make data-driven decisions to adapt their approach.

Processes and workflows must also be designed with adaptation in mind. Traditional waterfall methodologies, which rely on rigid, sequential phases, often struggle to accommodate change once development is underway. In contrast, iterative approaches like agile or lean development prioritize flexibility by breaking work into smaller increments that can be adjusted based on feedback. A team working in sprints, for example, can pivot quickly when priorities shift, delivering value incrementally rather than being locked into a months-long plan that may become obsolete. These adaptive workflows create a rhythm that allows teams to respond to change without losing momentum.

Collaboration across disciplines and roles strengthens a team's ability to adapt. Change rarely affects only one aspect of a project, and addressing it often requires input from developers, designers, product managers, and other stakeholders. Open communication ensures that everyone understands the implications of a change and can contribute their expertise to finding the best solution. For example, a decision to switch to a new database technology might involve not only backend developers but also operations teams responsible for deployment and monitoring. By fostering a culture of collaboration, teams can pool their knowledge and creativity to adapt more effectively.

Documentation and knowledge-sharing practices also play a vital role in adaptation strategies. When change occurs, teams must quickly understand the current state of the system and the context of the change. Clear, up-to-date documentation reduces the time spent deciphering existing code or processes, allowing teams to focus on implementing the necessary adjustments. Knowledge-sharing practices, such as pair programming, code reviews, or internal workshops, ensure that expertise is distributed across the team rather than siloed with specific individuals. This collective knowledge strengthens the team's resilience, as no single point of failure can derail progress during periods of change.

Resilience is closely tied to the ability to manage technical debt. While some level of technical debt is inevitable in any evolving system, unchecked debt can make adaptation increasingly difficult. For example, a codebase riddled with shortcuts, outdated dependencies, or poorly documented logic can become a significant obstacle when changes are required. Regularly addressing technical debt—whether through refactoring, updating dependencies, or improving test coverage—ensures that the system remains adaptable. This proactive approach prevents the accumulation of issues that could otherwise hinder progress when changes arise.

Another essential strategy is to prioritize automation wherever possible. Manual processes, while sometimes necessary, are often error-prone and time-consuming, making them ill-suited for handling frequent or complex changes. Automated testing, deployment pipelines, and infrastructure provisioning streamline repetitive tasks, allowing teams to focus on higher-level problem-solving. For example, a well-designed CI/CD pipeline can enable rapid iteration by ensuring that code changes are automatically tested and deployed in minutes rather than hours or days. This level of efficiency is critical for adapting to fast-paced environments where delays can compound and disrupt progress.

The human element of adaptation cannot be overlooked. Teams must be equipped with the skills and mindsets necessary to handle change effectively. Continuous learning and professional development are key components of this strategy. Encouraging team members to attend workshops, pursue certifications, or experiment with new technologies ensures that they remain versatile and capable of tackling emerging challenges. Additionally, fostering psychological safety within the team creates an environment where members feel comfortable voicing concerns, proposing ideas, and taking risks. This openness enables more innovative and effective adaptation, as diverse perspectives are considered and valued.

Adaptation strategies must also account for the broader context in which a system operates. External factors, such as market trends, regulatory changes, or competitor actions, often drive the need for adaptation. Staying informed about these dynamics allows teams to anticipate and prepare for changes rather than being caught off guard. For example, a shift in data privacy regulations might necessitate changes to how user information is stored and processed. Teams that monitor these developments and plan accordingly can implement changes smoothly, avoiding the last-minute scramble that often accompanies reactive responses.

Innovation Opportunities

Opportunities for innovation often emerge from the intersections of necessity and creativity. The ability to recognize and act on these opportunities is what distinguishes teams and organizations that merely survive from those that thrive. Innovation is not confined to groundbreaking inventions or sweeping industry disruptions; it also lies in subtle, incremental improvements that solve real problems, create efficiencies, or open doors to new possibilities. Identifying these opportunities requires a mindset that is attuned to change, a willingness to challenge assumptions, and the ability to connect disparate ideas in meaningful ways.

One of the most fertile grounds for innovation lies in addressing pain points. Challenges and inefficiencies within existing systems or workflows often signal areas ripe for improvement. A team struggling with long deployment times, for example, might identify an opportunity to streamline their processes through automation. Similarly, recurring user complaints about an application's interface could inspire a redesign that not only resolves the issues but also enhances the overall user experience. Pain points are not obstacles to be avoided; they are invitations to innovate. By observing where frustration arises—whether among developers, users, or stakeholders—teams can uncover opportunities to make meaningful changes that deliver value.

Innovation often emerges when existing tools or methods are applied in new contexts. Repurposing technology or techniques from one domain to solve problems in another can lead to unexpected breakthroughs. For instance, the principles of modular architecture, long used in software engineering, have inspired approaches to scalability and flexibility in hardware design. Similarly, the concept of version control, initially designed for managing code changes, has been adapted to fields like content creation and even legal document management. Looking beyond the immediate boundaries of a project or industry can reveal novel applications for familiar ideas, sparking innovation in the process.

Opportunities for innovation also arise from shifts in the external environment. Changes in technology, market demands, or regulatory frameworks often create new needs or possibilities. For example, the widespread adoption of mobile devices and the subsequent demand for responsive design revolutionized how developers approached web development. Similarly, the increasing emphasis on sustainability has driven innovation in energy-efficient computing and green data centers. Staying informed about these external developments allows teams to anticipate and capitalize on emerging trends rather than being left behind.

Collaboration is a powerful catalyst for innovation. Bringing together individuals with diverse skills, perspectives, and experiences fosters an environment where ideas can cross-pollinate. A designer may propose a user interface that inspires a developer to rethink the underlying architecture, or a product manager might highlight a market trend that leads to the creation of a new feature. The interplay of different viewpoints often results in solutions that no single individual could have conceived alone. Encouraging open communication and creating spaces for brainstorming and experimentation can unlock the collective creativity of a team.

Experimentation is central to discovering opportunities for innovation. Trying new approaches, even when the outcome is uncertain, often leads to insights that would not have been gained otherwise. Prototyping and iterative development are particularly effective in this regard, as they allow teams to test ideas quickly and refine them based on feedback. For example, a team experimenting with a new framework might discover not only its strengths but also its limitations, leading to the development of custom tools or extensions that enhance its functionality. The willingness to experiment—and to embrace failure as part of the learning process—is a hallmark of innovative teams.

Constraints, rather than being barriers to innovation, can actually drive it. Limited resources, tight deadlines, or specific requirements often force teams to think creatively and find solutions that would not have been considered under less restrictive conditions. For instance, a team tasked with building an application for low-bandwidth environments might develop highly efficient algorithms that later become a competitive advantage. Constraints focus attention and spark ingenuity, leading to solutions that are both effective and elegant.

User feedback is another rich source of innovation opportunities. Users often have a unique perspective on how a system or product is experienced in real-world conditions. Their input can reveal unmet needs, unexpected use cases, or areas where improvements could make a significant difference. Listening to users—whether through direct communication, surveys, or analytics—provides invaluable insights that can guide innovation efforts. For example, noticing that users frequently combine two features in unanticipated ways might inspire the creation of a new, integrated tool that simplifies their workflow.

Emerging technologies are a wellspring of possibilities for innovation. Advances in hardware, software, and connectivity continuously reshape what is possible, opening new doors for creative problem-solving. However, leveraging emerging technologies requires discernment. Not every new tool or approach is a good fit for every project. Teams must evaluate whether a technology aligns with their goals and whether it genuinely adds value. When applied thoughtfully, emerging technologies can enable breakthroughs that would have been impossible with older methods.

Organizational culture plays a critical role in fostering innovation. A culture that values curiosity, rewards experimentation, and encourages risk-taking creates an environment where opportunities for innovation are more likely to be recognized and pursued. Conversely, a culture that prioritizes adherence to established norms and punishes failure stifles creativity and discourages exploration. Leaders can promote a culture of innovation by celebrating successes, learning from failures, and providing the resources and support needed for teams to explore new ideas.

Timing is another crucial factor in innovation. Acting too early, before a technology or market is ready, can lead to wasted effort, while acting too late may mean missing an opportunity altogether. For example, early attempts at virtual reality in the 1990s failed due to limitations in hardware and consumer readiness. Decades later, advances in processing power, display technology, and user acceptance created the conditions for VR to become viable. Recognizing the right moment to act requires a combination of foresight, market awareness, and careful planning.

Lastly, innovation often begins with a simple question: "What if?" This question challenges assumptions and opens the door to possibilities that might otherwise be overlooked. What if a process could be automated? What if a feature could be simplified? What if a limitation could be eliminated? Asking these questions encourages teams to think beyond the status quo and imagine what could be achieved with the right ideas and effort.

Innovation is not a one-time event but an ongoing process. It thrives in environments where curiosity, collaboration, and experimentation are encouraged, and where challenges are viewed as opportunities rather than obstacles. By staying attuned to pain points, leveraging constraints, embracing user feedback, and exploring emerging technologies, teams can continuously uncover new opportunities to create value. Innovation is not just about creating something new; it is about making things better, solving problems, and finding ways to do more with less. It is the engine of progress and the key to staying relevant in a world that never stops changing.

www.ingramcontent.com/pod-product-compliance
Lightning Source LLC
LaVergne TN
LVHW050012050125
800368LV00017B/163